Killjoys

This publication is based on research that forms part of
the Paragon Initiative.

This five-year project will provide a fundamental reassessment
of what government should – and should not – do. It will put
every area of government activity under the microscope and
analyse the failure of current policies.

The project will put forward clear and considered solutions to
the UK's problems. It will also identify the areas of government
activity that can be put back into the hands of individuals,
families, civil society, local government, charities and markets.

The Paragon Initiative will create a blueprint for a better,
freer Britain – and provide a clear vision of a new relationship
between the state and society.

KILLJOYS

A Critique of Paternalism

CHRISTOPHER SNOWDON

Institute of
Economic Affairs

First published in Great Britain in 2017 by
The Institute of Economic Affairs
2 Lord North Street
Westminster
London SW1P 3LB
in association with London Publishing Partnership Ltd
www.londonpublishingpartnership.co.uk

The mission of the Institute of Economic Affairs is to improve understanding
of the fundamental institutions of a free society by analysing and expounding
the role of markets in solving economic and social problems.

A CIP catalogue record for this book is available from the British Library.

ISBN 978–0–255–36749-3

Many IEA publications are translated into languages other
than English or are reprinted. Permission to translate or to reprint
should be sought from the Director General at the address above.

Typeset in Kepler by T&T Productions Ltd
www.tandtproductions.com

Printed and bound in Great Britain by Page Bros

Please know I am quite aware of the hazards. I want to do it because I want to do it.

– Amelia Earhart

I shall not waste my days in trying to prolong them.

– Jack London

My only regret is that I have not drunk more champagne in my life.

– John Maynard Keynes

No one believes more firmly than Comrade Napoleon that all animals are equal. He would be only too happy to let you make your decisions for yourselves. But sometimes you might make the wrong decisions, comrades, and then where should we be?

– Squealer in *Animal Farm* (George Orwell)

CONTENTS

THE AUTHOR

Christopher Snowdon is the Head of Lifestyle Economics at the Institute of Economic Affairs. His research focuses on social freedoms, prohibition and policy-based evidence. He is a regular contributor to the *Spectator Health* blog and often appears on TV and radio discussing social and economic issues.

Snowdon is the editor of the Nanny State Index and the author of four books: *Selfishness, Greed and Capitalism* (2015), *The Art of Suppression* (2011), *The Spirit Level Delusion* (2010) and *Velvet Glove, Iron Fist* (2009). He has also written more than a dozen reports for the Institute of Economic Affairs including *Drinking, Fast and Slow, The Proof of the Pudding: Denmark's Fat Tax Fiasco, Cheap as Chips, Sock Puppets* and *Closing Time: Who's Killing the British Pub?*

FOREWORD

Doctors are inclined to get frustrated with patients who repeatedly turn up at their surgeries and clinics complaining of illnesses that are the direct result of their unhealthy lifestyles. In the past, they left it to the clergy to warn of the evils of gluttony, sloth and lust and to preach the virtues of sobriety and chastity. In recent times, as the influence of religion has waned, public health authorities have become the custodians of the new moral codes of healthy behaviour. Doctors feature prominently in campaigns to impose ever stricter bans and proscriptions on smoking, drinking alcohol and on foods rich in fats, sugars and salt in the hope that these measures will reduce demand for their services. At a conference of the British Medical Association in July 2017, doctors' outrage over recent outbreaks of measles was expressed in a resolution condemning 'anti-vaxxers who deny immunisations to their children'.[1] As a result, the BMA leadership is reviewing its established opposition to mandatory immunisation policies.

---

1   Tom Moberly, UK doctors mull mandatory vaccination, BMJ: 22 July 2017, p. 140. BMJ2017; 358:j3414.

As Christopher Snowdon argues in this timely book, there are good grounds, both pragmatic and principled, for resisting the trend towards more paternalistic public health policies. Though public health advocates claim their policies are 'evidence-based', Snowdon shows that much of this evidence is selective and contentious. Paternalism, he argues, intrudes upon autonomy, 'drains vitality' and deprives the individual of experience in decision-making. Whereas classical political economy assumed the competence and rationality of a reasonably well-informed consumer, all these assumptions are now questioned by the gurus of behavioural economics and the mandarins of the new public health.

In response to criticisms of public health measures as steps towards a 'nanny state', the Nuffield Council on Bioethics has proclaimed an alternative 'stewardship model'.[2] From this perspective, the state, rather than behaving in an intrusive and authoritarian manner, assumes a caretaker role, taking responsibility for protecting vulnerable people. The quiet expansion of the category of vulnerability is the key to the appeal of the stewardship model to public health authorities.

In his famous *On Liberty* (1859), discussed in detail here, John Stuart Mill exempted children from his strictures against paternalism: he considered it appropriate that the state, like parents, should treat children, well, as children.

---

2   Nuffield Council on Bioethics, Public Health: Ethical Issues, November 2007, pp. xvi–xvii.

The Nuffield Council immediately extends this category to include 'young people'. At a time when many are proposing the extension of the franchise to 16-year-olds, it endorses the government's decision to increase the minimum age at which tobacco products can be bought from 16 to 18. It also, without explanation, includes 'the elderly' as a vulnerable category, bringing the proportion regarded as needing state protection on grounds of age alone up to around 40 per cent.[3]

As we proceed through the Nuffield Council report, the ranks of the vulnerable in need of protection continue to swell. The Council briskly adds 'the socially disadvantaged', people of 'low socio-economic status', who are known to suffer poorer health.[4] The proportion of the population judged officially to be living in relative poverty is 18 per cent. It includes people who are 'lacking the capacity to make informed decisions', such as those with learning disabilities or serious mental illness. It also includes those who lack capacity because of 'other factors that contribute to a lack of autonomy', such as addictions to nicotine (most smokers, around 20 per cent of the population) and alcohol ('hazardous drinkers' are estimated at 18 per cent). These addictions justify the intervention of the 'stewardship state' because they impose on sufferers 'physiological, psychological and social barriers that

---

3   Ibid., p. 144.

4   Ibid.

restrict their ability to change behaviour and may hinder permanent changes'.[5]

In a truly Orwellian conclusion, the Nuffield Council adds to the list of the vulnerable 'those without sufficient healthcare-related knowledge to act as fully autonomous citizens'.[6] The 'stewardship state' thus extends its protective embrace over an inexorably growing proportion of the population. This starts from those deemed incapable on grounds of immaturity or senility, stretches to include the relatively impoverished as well as those disqualified on grounds of mental or moral incapacity and finally extends to those judged (presumably by the public health authorities) too ignorant or stupid to know what is good for their own health. The 'stewardship state' grows in power and authority in proportion to the degradation of the subjective capacities of its people.

There is an ominous parallel between the concept of the vulnerable individual in the sphere of health and that of the incompetent citizen in the sphere of politics. On one hand, a substantial proportion of the population is judged so incapable of pursuing its own interests in the sphere of health that it needs official 'stewardship'. On the other, critics of popular democracy suggest that a similar proportion lacks sufficient 'politics-related' knowledge to act as fully autonomous citizens in the processes of democratic decision-making.

---

5   Ibid., p. 107.
6   Ibid., p. 144.

Meanwhile, back in the surgery, doctors are likely to encounter the objects of these paternalistic policies as individuals who have been infantilised and patronised and deprived of respect and autonomy. Paternalistic public health measures are destined to foster dependency and increase the burden of ill-health on both individuals and society.

DR MICHAEL FITZPATRICK

Michael Fitzpatrick is a former GP.
He is the author of The Tyranny of Health:
Doctors and the Regulation of Lifestyle, 2000.

August 2017

1 PATERNALISM AND LIBERALISM

Every day, people do things of which others disapprove. They do things that might seem unwise or immoral. They do things that are unhealthy or dangerous. They do things they might regret. This is a book about what happens when the government tries to stop them.

In recent decades, government paternalism has switched its focus from public morality to public health. Religion has lost its hold over politics. Free speech is far from absolute but blasphemy laws are no more and it is half a century since theatrical productions had to be approved by the Lord Chamberlain. Today, paternalist or 'nanny state' regulation attempts to reduce the consumption of legal products that can have a negative effect on the health of the user if consumed in excess or over a period of many years. The usual targets are alcohol, tobacco, 'junk food' and sugary drinks, with e-cigarettes and gambling products sometimes thrown into the mix.

Regulatory responses range from warning labels to full prohibition, with typical policies including sin taxes, marketing bans and sale restrictions, all aimed at curtailing what paternalists call 'the Three As': Affordability, Availability and Advertising. Mandatory product reformulation, graphic warnings, bans on branding and minimum pricing are also part of the armoury.

Most governments can implement any or all of these policies, but should they? Increasingly, it is *assumed* that something must be done. It is *assumed* that the state should act if people are eating more sugar than is recommended or drinking more alcohol than government guidelines advise. By definition, guidelines and recommendations imply free choice and yet the message from health campaigners is that the state cannot rest until everyone has complied with them.

A demand for something to be done can morph into a demand for *anything* to be done. Faced with a series of supposed crises and epidemics – the binge-drinking crisis, the obesity epidemic, etc. – the government is told to take action at all costs. But taking action at all costs is a terrible way to make policy. Even a country fighting a war of national survival would not disregard all costs in the hope of making progress. Why, then, should the weighing of costs and benefits go out of the window when it comes to lifestyle regulation?

In practice, governments are not usually run by zealots and the political choice is rarely between complete prohibition and total laissez-faire. Few people deny the need for some form of regulation. The question is whether regulation should be designed to protect people from themselves. Before answering that question, you might want to hear the specifics of each case. What is the person doing? How great is the risk? What are the benefits? Many people are prepared to accept a degree of government paternalism in some areas but not in others.

Or you might answer according to your philosophy. Perhaps you feel that people are not always capable of making their own decisions and that the combined wisdom of experts should take precedence. Alternatively, you may feel that liberty is sacrosanct and that individuals must be free to choose so long as other people do not suffer from their choices. The latter position is a crude summation of John Stuart Mill's stance on individual liberty, and it is with Mill that we will begin.

The liberal view

It is almost impossible to start any discussion of paternalism without mentioning Mill's famous 'harm principle', which places a limit on government intervention in human behaviour. The principle, wrote Mill (1987: 68), is that

> the sole end for which mankind are warranted, individually or collectively, in interfering with the liberty of action of any of their number, is self-protection. That the only purpose for which power can be rightfully exercised over any member of a civilised community, against his will, is to prevent harm to others. His own good, either physical or moral, is not a sufficient warrant. He cannot rightfully be compelled to do or forbear because it will be better for him to do so, because it will make him happier, because, in the opinion of others, to do so would be wise, or even right.

When these words were first published in 1859 the doctrine of individual liberty was not new, but it was Mill who laid it out in the 'most comprehensive, extensive, and systematic form' (Himmelfarb 1987: 9). There is a clarity of thought in *On Liberty* that makes the concepts seem simpler than they are. Mill himself described his golden rule as 'one very simple principle' but generations of scholars have found it to be anything but. There is limitless disagreement about the meaning and application of the harm principle. Yet its fundamental idea – that government is justified in protecting people from others but never from themselves – resonated in Victorian Britain and still resonates today. To a large extent, it is this belief that distinguishes liberal democracies from states which require the individual to be subsumed by the religious, collectivist or nationalist beliefs of their rulers.

Even those who have no appetite for liberty understand that the concept of freedom has an enduring appeal. Mussolini paid lip service to it in *The Doctrine of Fascism* when he wrote (Mussolini and Gentile 1932: 17):

> In our state the individual is not deprived of freedom. In fact, he has greater liberty than an isolated man, because the state protects him and he is part of the state.

We will not waste too many words on disingenuous dictators except to note that *Il Duce* felt obliged to redefine the concept of freedom rather than dismiss it entirely. Nobody wishes to be regarded as a freedom-hater and few people self-identify as paternalists or nanny statists. Those who breach the harm principle usually do so by distorting the concept of liberty or by arguing that Mill's arguments do not apply to their own time and place. Most people innately feel that adults should be afforded a great deal of autonomy. In a 2014 ComRes poll, 70 per cent of respondents agreed that 'individuals should be responsible for their own lifestyle choices and the government should not intervene'. Only 21 per cent thought that 'there should be more government regulation to stop people making unhealthy lifestyle choices' (ComRes 2014). We believe, in theory at least, that people should live and let live.

An analysis of Mill's philosophy is beyond the reach of this book, but a few points that are relevant to our topic of paternalism should be raised. There is much debate about the meaning of 'harm' as Mill uses it in *On Liberty*, but it is clear that he did not intend it to be defined so broadly as to include the psychological impact of taking offence, feeling sad or being bereaved. If we were to include such emotions as harm, it would allow far more government intervention than Mill would have countenanced. The mere knowledge that an irreligious or risky activity is taking place somewhere in the world could be enough to distress a moral puritan. When Mill wrote about harm, he meant only direct harm to an individual's person or property.

A more interesting question is whether individual liberty is as important as Mill believed. He assumed that society would be better off if people made their own choices, unencumbered by the tyranny of majority opinion, but not everybody has been convinced. For Mill, freedom, originality, eccentricity and genius are indivisible. Genius cannot thrive without the oxygen of liberty, he argues, and 'the amount of eccentricity in a society has generally been proportional to the amount of genius, mental vigour, and moral courage it contained' (Mill 1987: 132). This *could* be true but it looks rather like a bald assertion, as does Mill's claim that 'the chief danger' of his time was that 'so few dare to be eccentric'. It is not obvious that eccentricity *per se* has any great benefit to society and it could be argued that exceptional genius is not the product of the environment but of genetics and education. In any case, genius and eccentricity can tolerate many petty regulations before being suppressed. Isaiah Berlin (1969: 128) argued that 'love of truth and fiery individualism grow at least as often in severely disciplined communities, among, for example, the puritan Calvinists of Scotland or New England, or under military discipline, as in more tolerant or indifferent societies'.

To have 'persons of genius', says Mill, 'it is necessary to preserve the soil in which they grow' (Mill 1987: 129). The assumption that promoting liberty will foster originality – and therefore progress – is plausible but speculative. It is not, in itself, strong enough to validate the harm principle. It seems here as if Mill is trying to tempt the average reader, whom he suspects of being intolerant and conformist, with the promise of benefits from allowing others to lead unusual lifestyles. In so doing, Mill puts himself in the position of having to argue that *any* regulation that breaches the harm principle reduces the sum total of genius in a nation, and yet it is not at all obvious that, to take a contemporary example of paternalism, forcing people to wear seat belts has any such effect. Mill might argue that even trivial encroachments on freedom stifle originality by creating a hostile intellectual climate – he talks about genius only being able to 'breathe freely in an *atmosphere* of freedom' (emphasis in the original) – but this applies more to free speech than to some of the regulatory questions he addresses, such as whether poisons should be sold over the counter.

Mill is more convincing when he argues that paternalism drains people of their vitality by making decisions for them. Relieved of the need to think for themselves, Mill feared that they would stop thinking at all, until 'by dint of not following their own nature they have no nature to follow' (ibid.: 126). It might also be argued that a society that bans so much on grounds of safety lulls individuals into believing that everything that is legal is safe; that legality itself amounts to tacit encouragement (Miller 2010: 152). In this way, paternalism hinders our ability to make good decisions, first by giving us too little practice and then by giving us unrealistic expectations.

In my view, Mill's simplest and strongest case for individual liberty arrives a few pages later when he writes that a person's 'own mode of laying out his existence is the best, not because it is the best in itself, but because it is his own mode' (Mill 1987: 133). Since people have different tastes and preferences, it is undesirable for others, even if they are the majority, to impose foreign preferences upon them. Hospers (1980: 265) puts it another way, saying 'what is for *the person's good* may not be the same as *what he wants*' (emphasis in the original). Citing the example of a drug addict who wants nothing in life but 'drug-soaked euphoria', he continues (emphasis in the original):

Even if *we* believe, and even if we believe truly, that such a life does not serve *his* good – we think of the wasted talents and what he might have achieved and enjoyed if he had not (in our view) thrown away his life – we are nevertheless faced with the fact that *what we want for him* is not the same as *what he wants for himself.*

In the final analysis, Hospers concludes that we must say to ourselves:

It's his life, and I don't own it. I may sometimes use coercion against his will to promote his own ends, but I must never use coercion against his will to promote *my* ends. From my point of view, and perhaps even in some cosmic perspective, my ideals for him are better than his own. But his have the unique distinguishing feature that they are *his*; and as such, I have no right to interfere forcibly with him.

Mill does not explicitly state his case in terms of equity or anti-discrimination, but he is clearly motivated by a desire to protect minorities. In a democracy, majorities seldom need protection. It is not necessary to argue that the majority will benefit from leaving the minority alone – though they might – it is enough to know that the minorities are able to pursue happiness in their own way. Mill may have been right in his assumption that an atmosphere of freedom fosters creativity and ultimately benefits the whole society, but the case for liberty does not depend on there being spillover effects for other people.

The dominant and recurring theme in *On Liberty* is Mill's belief that Britain was sinking under a tide of conformity and 'collective mediocrity' (Mill 1987: 131). An exceptional and unorthodox individual himself, Mill argued that the average man has average tastes and little sympathy for free thinkers and non-conformists. If left unrestrained, he saw democracy becoming nothing more than a vehicle for the prejudices of the masses. 'The likings and dislikings of society, or of some powerful portion of it,' he wrote, 'are thus the main thing which has practically determined the rules laid down for general observance, under the penalties of law or opinion' (ibid.: 66). He berated his fellow intellectuals for spending time discussing 'what things society ought to like or dislike' instead of asking the more fundamental question of whether society's 'likings and dislikings should be a law to individuals' (ibid.). *On Liberty* answers that question with an emphatic 'no'.

2　THE CLASSICAL ECONOMIST'S VIEW

On the utilitarian scales balancing society's pleasure and pain, Mill's principle allows the minority to pursue fulfilment without causing pain to others. The net effect on human happiness can only be positive. This is the crossroads at which utilitarianism, liberalism and economics meet; hardly surprising since Mill was a utilitarian, a liberal and an economist. In standard economic theory, it is assumed that an individual will attempt to maximise his utility. Mill is quick to note that there is no objective measure of what is best for an individual, but so long as the person is equipped with 'a tolerable amount of common sense and experience' we must assume that the life he has chosen for himself, within the constraints of his own circumstances and abilities, is more to his liking than the life that would be chosen for him by a committee, a king, or his peers (ibid.: 132–33). Only through liberty, therefore, can the individual maximise his utility.

Economics can be used to justify regulation of risky activities, up to and including prohibition, but not on the basis of paternalism. Like Mill, economists assume that individuals will use their freedom and resources to pursue the best life for themselves *as judged by themselves*. If we want to know people's preferences, we only have to observe what they do when they have the freedom to choose. If they are prevented from acting freely, they will be less able to maximise their utility and more likely to suffer a welfare loss.

There is no assumption in economics that people will make the 'best' choices according to some objective standard. The real question is whether somebody else – in practice, a politician – would make better choices for them. It is doubtful that he would. One reason for this was explained by Mill when he noted that 'the most ordinary man or woman has means of knowledge immeasurably surpassing those that can be possessed by anyone else' (Mill 1987: 143). Bureaucrats do not know what the individual's tastes, desires and goals are. Lacking adequate information, the government can only work on 'general presumptions which may be altogether wrong and, even if right, are as likely as not to be misapplied to individual cases' (ibid.). As a result, Mill says, 'the odds are that it interferes wrongly and in the wrong place' (ibid.: 151).

Feinberg (1971: 109–10) suggests that individuals take up to five factors into account when making a risky decision, namely:

1. The probability of harming oneself.
2. The severity of the harm.
3. The probability of achieving the goal for which one is putting oneself at risk.
4. The importance of that goal.
5. The necessity of incurring the risk to achieve the goal.

These five judgements amount to one big trade-off between costs and benefits. A paternalistic government may or may not be better able to assess the statistical likelihoods of (1) and (3), and it may be able to provide information on (2) and (5), but only the individual can make the value judgement involved in (4), and only the individual knows how much risk he is prepared to tolerate. Even if the state could accurately quantify the severity of harm (2) and the probability of the person coming to harm (1), only the individual could make the value judgement involved in weighing up all five factors to come to a final decision. It may be that the government has better access to – or better understanding of – information that could help the individual make the decision, but on several crucial points the government knows next to nothing.

Economists have long understood that the wide dispersion of knowledge in society fatally undermines attempts at central planning (Hayek 1945). Taken individually, people have limited knowledge but, by interacting in the market, millions of people are able to direct resources more efficiently than a system that abolishes markets and has no price mechanism to guide it. Economists therefore assume that 'the operation of free markets maximises social welfare' and that so long as markets are working efficiently 'government intervention can only decrease social welfare' (Cawley 2011: 128–29).

Assuming the individual to be of sound mind, reasonably well informed and making decisions of his own free will, Feinberg concludes that interference can only be justified if 'the risk is extreme and, in respect to its objectively assessable components, manifestly unreasonable' (Feinberg 1971: 110). He offers several examples to illustrate what he means by 'extreme', such as chopping off one's own hand, selling oneself into permanent slavery, and taking a drug that provides an hour's pleasure but is certain to be followed by a violently painful death. These activities are so extraordinarily self-destructive as to create the strong presumption that the person is not of sound mind. The fact that the examples are extremely unusual, if not wholly hypothetical, is prima facie evidence that they are irrational. By contrast, the billions of people who are prepared to risk their long-term health with tobacco, alcohol, food or physical inactivity make it very difficult to portray such behaviours as 'manifestly unreasonable'.

But there is a major caveat to classical economists' laissez-faire approach to lifestyle regulation. If there are market failures, government action can be justified – so long as it will lead to better outcomes. The aim of such regulation is not to change people's behaviour, let alone their preferences. It is not designed to make people healthier or to make them better citizens. It is designed only to ensure that resources are allocated as efficiently as possible given consumers' preferences. Relevant market failures for our purposes include those which create information asymmetries, such as inaccurate labelling and false advertising, and negative externalities, such as financial costs forced onto unwilling third parties.

For market exchanges to optimise social wellbeing, consumers should be reasonably well informed and of sound mind. It goes without saying that paternalism is appropriate in the case of children and the same is true of those who are incapable of giving informed consent as a result of senility, insanity or brain-damage.[1] Hospers (1980) agrees that government paternalism is difficult to justify when adults are making voluntary decisions, but questions whether consent is meaningful if the individual is threatened with coercion or punishment, is poorly informed about the consequences, or is in an unhealthy psychological state.

People can be persuaded to buy a product through sales patter or advertising but the mere fact that they would not have bought the product without these influences does not mean that their choice was involuntary. Many factors can be influences – or 'nudges' – without being coercive, but it is less clear whether somebody who has been conned into believing that a bottle of snake oil will cure their rheumatism has made a truly voluntary choice. If the buyer is deliberately misled with false information, or if an important piece of information is deliberately concealed, then the market has arguably failed since the buyer would have made a different choice if he had been equipped with the facts. It is for the law to decide where salesmanship ends and fraud begins, but the logic behind such laws is uncontroversial.

We shall return to the issue of persuasion in a later chapter. For now let us conclude that economists believe that markets produce the best outcomes if competition exists and if choices are voluntary. For this, consumers must be reasonably well informed and reasonably rational. Like

---

1   After describing the harm principle in *On Liberty*, Mill's very next sentence reads: 'It is, perhaps, hardly necessary to say that this doctrine is meant to apply only to human beings in the maturity of their faculties' (Mill 1987: 69).

John Stuart Mill, mainstream economists assume that the average consumer is basically rational, which is to say he generally acts in accordance with his preferences. However, some paternalists argue that findings from behavioural economics prove that people are intractably irrational and, therefore, require more government paternalism than has traditionally been assumed. The following chapters will discuss the philosophical and economic arguments in favour of 'nudge' (soft) paternalism, coercive (hard) paternalism, and 'public health' paternalism.

3   SOFT PATERNALISM AND NUDGE THEORY

Economists have never really believed that people are ruthlessly self-interested, perfectly informed robots who are constantly balancing costs against benefits. There are not enough hours in the day for us to be perfectly informed about every decision we make and so we use shortcuts (*heuristics*) to help us reach an outcome that might not be perfect, but is good enough (*satisficing*). We use rules of thumb and best estimates. We rely on recommendations from friends, and trust brands that have served us well in the past. 'It makes far more sense to say that people display bounded rationality than to accuse them of "irrationality"' says Sunstein (2014a: 11). This is not necessarily a bad thing. It is perfectly rational to settle for less than best if it saves us time and effort, particularly when the costs are low. It would be unreasonable to spend a day researching which box of matches to buy, but it could be time well spent if we were buying a house.

But what if our mental shortcuts and human frailties stop us getting what we really want? Since the 1970s, the field of behavioural economics has shown that people fall foul of a number of cognitive biases which lead to bad decision-making. These subtle but common irrational responses have been said to undermine John Stuart Mill's faith in reason and justify a new wave of paternalism.

'Soft paternalism' went mainstream in 2008 when Richard Thaler and Cass Sunstein published their influential best-seller, *Nudge*. In it they argue that inertia, in particular, exerts a powerful influence over people. If one option requires conscious effort while the other doesn't, we are more likely to do nothing and settle for the default. And yet the default option does not necessarily reflect our preference when we are asked directly (that is, in a yes/no question with no default option).

For example, most people express a wish to be an organ donor and yet millions of people never get around to seeking out the relevant form and filling it in. Economists are wary of taking people's stated preferences too seriously – talk is cheap – but in this instance, we can assume that most people's desire to be an organ donor is genuine. Many stated preferences, such as the desire to emigrate or drink less, are derailed by the sacrifices required to bring them to fruition, but with organ donation there is no real sacrifice because the person will be dead when it happens. Wanting to donate one's organs is therefore unlikely to be a 'second-order preference'. People are not saying that they wish they were the kind of person who wanted to be an organ donor; they have just never had sufficient incentive to make the arrangements. They are putting off until tomorrow what they could do today.[1]

---

1 There may also be a cognitive bias in people discounting the possibility that they are going to die in the near future, but that is a different issue. If the people who died at a young age (when their organs are most valuable) knew that they would die young, they would presumably be more likely to fill out the form in time.

It has been suggested that governments should flip the default option by introducing 'presumed consent' for organ donations. This would make human organs available for transplant unless the deceased person had explicitly said that he or she did not want to be a donor. Changing the default option has a huge effect on uptake. Thaler and Sunstein (2008: 188) report the results of an experiment in which 82 per cent of participants agreed to become donors when they had to opt out whereas only 42 per cent became donors when they had to opt in.

Presumed consent has two advantages: it would bring many people's actions in line with their preferences and it would save lives. However, just as inertia and procrastination lead to too few people becoming organ donors under a system of explicit consent, the same biases would probably lead to too many people becoming organ donors under a system of presumed consent. Some people with religious or other beliefs which forbid them from donating their organs will fail to fill in the relevant forms. This makes presumed consent a tricky ethical issue, particularly since some people are uncomfortable with the idea of the state presuming ownership of their bodies, alive or dead.

Fortunately, there is a third way that seems to do the job. In the above experiment, 79 per cent of participants agreed to be donors if they were given a straight choice with no default option. This suggests that all that needs to be done is to get the question under people's noses rather than wait for them to visit a website or pick up a form. Thaler and Sunstein recommend adding the question to driving licence application and renewal forms. This will reach most adults and it has the added, though macabre, advantage of reaching two groups who are particularly likely to leave young, fresh organs to harvest: motorcyclists and newly qualified motorists. This third way is perfectly libertarian and it is debatable whether even the second way (presumed consent) is illiberal, since people are free to opt out. Either way, it illustrates how default options can affect our behaviour.

Inertia is just one of the cognitive biases that lead to suboptimal decision-making. Thaler and Sunstein marshall an impressive array of evidence showing that people's actions can be significantly affected by seemingly minor details in what they call the 'choice architecture'. Given that default options are inevitable, Thaler and Sunstein argue that they should be designed to 'influence choices in a way that will make choosers better off, *as judged by themselves*' (ibid.: 5 – emphasis in original).

Behavioural experiments have shown the effectiveness of all sorts of interventions in the choice architecture. Painting a picture of a fly on a urinal gives men something to aim at and reduces 'spillage'. Automatic enrolment of employees into pension plans (with an easy opt-out for those who don't want to join) increases uptake and gives people more savings in later life. Sending people a letter telling them that their money is needed for 'vital public services' makes them more likely to pay their income tax bill on time. Getting a patient to write down the details of their doctor's appointment (rather than having a member of staff do it) makes them less likely to forget about it. Placing healthy food at the front of the counter in cafeterias makes it more likely to be picked up. Even putting a light above the fruit bowl can significantly increase the number of people who opt for fruit in school canteens (Wansink 2015).

If liberty is defined as the 'absence of legal coercion' (Feinberg 1984: 7), it is difficult to argue that any of these interventions are illiberal. Thaler and Sunstein lay out clear criteria for nudging to ensure that freedom of choice is respected. They define a nudge (Thaler and Sunstein 2008: 6) as a change to

> any aspect of the choice architecture that alters people's behaviour in a predictable way without forbidding any options or significantly changing their economic incentives.

In other words, the nudge must be evidence-based ('alters people's behaviour in a predictable way'), cannot involve bans ('without forbidding any options') and cannot make the activity less enjoyable or more expensive ('[without] significantly changing their economic incentives').

Nudge theory has been criticised for being manipulative (Glaeser 2006) but, as Thaler and Sunstein repeatedly point out, it is no more manipulative than any other attempt by governments, businesses and individuals to influence our decisions. Choice architecture is everywhere and eradicating defaults is not an option. The criticism that nudging is manipulative implies that there is some sort of natural choice architecture with which the government is meddling but, as Sunstein (2014a: 140) points out, when default options exist it is 'not because God or nature has so decreed' but because somebody has chosen them. For nudge theorists, it is better if the architecture helps us follow our desires rather than dragging us away from them. School canteens have to place the food somewhere, so why not place the healthier food at the front? It would be no less 'manipulative' to place it at the back. Similarly, it is not obvious why an automatic opt-out of a pension plan is less manipulative than an automatic opt-in.

Businesses use nudge tactics all the time. Online subscriptions are often renewed unless we explicitly cancel them and libertarians have no problem with this because consumers are free to take their business elsewhere. The market will ultimately punish any company that gets a reputation for sharp practice. It could be argued that people expect a degree of manipulation and salesmanship from business but would feel patronised if the government used the same tricks in an effort to save us from ourselves. Hausman and Welch (2010: 131) suggest that 'the cacophony of invocations of irrational responses by non-governmental agents' is made tolerable by 'the limits to its effectiveness and the extent to which these invocations conflict with one another and cancel one another out.' By contrast, exploitation of psychological foibles by monopolistic government is 'a form of disrespectful social control' (ibid.: 134).

Since Thaler and Sunstein insist that nudging should be done openly and with full publicity, it is certainly possible that some people will feel humiliated and browbeaten by the knowledge that government is subtly influencing their personal decisions. In the view of Isaiah Berlin (1969: 157):

benefit toilet cleaners rather than toilet users. The beneficiary of organ donations is the live recipient, not the dead donor. A reminder to pay one's income tax could benefit the individual if it helps avoid a fine, but the main beneficiary is the tax office. Reminders, warnings and education are not paternalistic because, as Hausman and Welch (2010: 127) note, 'providing information and giving advice treats individuals as fully competent decision makers.' Nudges of this sort may well help people pursue their goals but that does not necessarily make them paternalistic. They can be justified by mainstream economics.

The British government has been experimenting with behavioural economics since 2010 when the Behavioural Insights Team was set up under David Cameron. Popularly known as the Nudge Unit, it began life with the commendable pledge to close itself down if it did not produce a tenfold return on its £500,000 start-up costs. In his book *Inside the Nudge Unit*, the team's director David Halpern describes a string of nudging successes which only serve to demonstrate the limits of 'libertarian paternalism'. The most significant of them include adding a note to income tax reminders telling the recipient that 'most people pay their tax on time'; adding a photo of the driver's car to unpaid car tax bills; sending debtors a text message to tell them that the bailiffs are due to appear on their doorstep; and offering people a loft clearance service to increase uptake of subsidised home insulation (Halpern 2015: 3–4).[2]

---

2   The Behavioural Insights Team realised that the hassle of clearing out their lofts was a bigger deterrent to people than the cost of roof insulation.

All these nudges had the desired effect and, Halpern says, brought in tens of millions of pounds. Since they cost little to implement, they were worthwhile innovations but most of them relied on little more than a change in presentation. Only the loft clearance scheme was paternalistic (the others were principally for the benefit of the government), but it was not really a 'nudge' since it changed the costs and benefits, and it was not libertarian because it forced taxpayers to pay for other people's home improvements.

The most damning criticism of the nudge project is not that it is illiberal, but that it is insubstantial in the context of the big issues facing government. If one strips out all the nudges that are not paternalistic, not libertarian and not trivial, there is little left of the libertarian paternalist agenda. It is precisely because Thaler and Sunstein are reluctant to use state coercion that the implications of nudge theory for public policy are so limited. There are plenty of nudges that can be adopted by businesses and individuals and yet nudging in its pure form – with the caveat that the nudge should be easy to ignore or avoid – has fewer practical applications for government. Nudges can be effective in reminding people to do things, but they do not offer solutions to the major political challenges of the day, and the assurance of a hassle-free opt-out will never satisfy single-issue campaigners who see bigger gains to be made from compulsion.

The truth is that most governments are more paternalistic and less libertarian than the nudge theorists. If the principles of *Nudge* were rolled out across government, many existing laws would have to be repealed and few new laws would be made. From a libertarian perspective, it is unfortunate that Thaler and Sunstein do not apply their principles to such issues as gambling and narcotics, where US law goes far beyond subtle nudges. One can only speculate as to what legislative programme would emerge if a society was started from scratch based on nudge theory, but it would surely be more libertarian than any country currently in existence.

One concern about the nudge agenda is that it creates a slippery slope of regulation, with government becoming gradually more intrusive and manipulative. In its pure form, this should not be possible since Thaler and Sunstein's criteria preclude the use of coercion, but critics were given ammunition in 2014 when Cass Sunstein went solo to write a follow-up book, *Why Nudge?*, which took a notably less libertarian line. Applying a new golden rule, Sunstein maintained that 'nudges are usually the best response' but added that 'harder forms of paternalism are not off-limits' (Sunstein 2014a: 17, 142). It may or may not be relevant that Sunstein had taken a job as the 'Regulatory Czar' in the US government between writing *Nudge* and *Why Nudge?*, but whatever the reason for his change in tone, the newfound embrace of hard paternalism undermined the intellectual coherence of the nudge philosophy. Sunstein now supports hard paternalism 'when the benefits justify the costs' (ibid.).

The introduction of a vague cost–benefit analysis involving 'social welfare' compromises the relative clarity of nudge theory by opening the door to paternalists making value judgements on other people's behalf. It is hard to imagine Mill adding a footnote to his harm principle saying 'unless the benefits outweigh the costs, in which case co-ercion is not off-limits'.[3] Costs and benefits can never be properly quantified when dealing with pleasure, pain, joy and remorse. The judgement can only be made by the individual who is going to experience the benefits and pay the costs. Any valuation by a third party is likely to be biased and arbitrary.

A principle that boils down to opposing government coercion unless the benefits outweigh the costs *in the eyes of those who are not involved in the transaction* is no principle at all. In contrast with Thaler and Sunstein's original nudge criteria and Mill's harm principle, it does not allow a line to be drawn between appropriate and excessive interventions. In practice, it would allow any number of illiberal intrusions so long as they achieved the paternalist's goal and did not come with too many negative side effects. This leads us into the realm of coercive paternalism, which is the subject of our next chapter.

---

3   Mill does make one exception to his principle, albeit for a self-regarding action that is extremely rare if not non-existent. He says that nobody should be allowed to sell themselves into permanent slavery. Feinberg (1971) argues that he was wrong to do so.

4 COERCIVE PATERNALISM

Few people are prepared to define themselves as coercive paternalists. An exception is Sarah Conly, whose 2013 book *Against Autonomy: Justifying Coercive Paternalism* is unusual in making the case for the nanny state openly and honestly. An American professor of philosophy who has since written a book arguing that people do not have the right to have more than one child (Conly 2016), Conly builds on the same claims about intractable irrationality found in *Nudge*, but argues that the force of law should be employed to prevent individuals making risky decisions even if they are well informed about the hazards. It is not enough to give people nudges they can opt out of, she says, because the right to opt out will not only be used by those who have made a rational and informed decision, it will also be used by those who would, in her view, benefit from being nudged.

'More freedom to choose', Conly says, 'means more people will choose badly' (Conly 2013: 31). Therefore, it is time to turn to 'a better approach, which is simply to save people from themselves by making certain courses of action illegal. We should, for example, ban cigarettes; ban trans fats; require restaurants to reduce portion sizes to less elephantine dimensions; increase required savings, and control how much debt individuals can run up' (Conly 2013: 1). Conly does not shy away from the philosophical and practical objections to her brand of hard paternalism. Because she makes her case eloquently, *Against Autonomy* offers an opportunity to put Mill's philosophy up against a serious thinker from the opposite side.

At the core of Mill's view of individual liberty is the belief that people are best placed to make their own decisions because they have both the incentive and knowledge to make the optimal choices *given their own preferences*. In *Principles of Political Economy*, he wrote that 'people understand their own business and their interests better, and care for them more, than the government does, or can be expected to do' (Mill 2004: 282). Tastes vary and what may seem a rational choice to one person will seem crazy to another. Given the plurality of individual desires, Mill argued, there is no case for allowing the heavy hand of the state to make prohibitions unless the activity in question directly harms other people without their consent.

Sarah Conly rejects this. She argues that people are united behind certain universal goals which some of us fail to achieve as a result of cognitive biases and human weakness. Autonomy is overrated, she says, when it leads us to do things we will regret. Given her more authoritarian approach, the challenge for Conly is twofold. First, she must find universal human goals to which everyone subscribes. Second, she must find effective ways for the government to coerce people into achieving those goals. It is imperative that effective and harmless methods are found because, unlike nudge paternalism, coercive paternalism cannot be opted out of and will apply to all. Furthermore, it should not disadvantage those who have minority tastes and should not become a runaway train of authoritarianism. As we shall see, this is a difficult circle to square.

The mirage of universal goals

A *means paternalist* is interested in helping people achieve their own goals whereas as an *ends paternalist* dictates what their goals should be and uses government intervention to direct people towards them. Sunstein and Thaler present themselves as means paternalists. They accept that people have different goals and preferences, but argue that individuals would make different – and probably better – decisions if the choice architecture was not working against them. This can be tested empirically. As mentioned above, many people make a different decision about organ donation and pension plans if they are given a neutral question rather than an automatic opt-in or opt-out.

Conly also claims to be a means paternalist, but much of her argument resembles ends paternalism. 'The paternalist wants to make people better off,' writes Conly, 'and if we have an idea of what constitutes objective well-being, it seems reasonable to think the paternalist would impose this on people, even though we really don't want this' (ibid.: 107).[1] Conly focuses on two areas of 'objective well-being'

---

1   This seems to contradict a statement elsewhere in her book in which she says 'I do not argue that there are objectively good ends' (ibid.: 43).

which she believes are suitable candidates for 'laws that force people to do what is good for them' (ibid.: 3). These are health and financial security. Put simply, she argues that everybody wishes to be alive and everybody wants to be financially secure, therefore coercive government action that helps people to fulfil these ambitions is justified. If there are other universal goals that justify hard paternalism, Conly does not mention them in *Against Autonomy*, and even her goals for health do not, in practice, extend beyond not smoking and not being obese. To this end, she proposes a ban on cigarettes and various interventions in the food supply.

Her examples of objective well-being are uncontroversial on the face of it. It is trivially true to say that people would sooner be healthy than sick and would prefer to be affluent in old age than poor. These things are clearly important. The problem is that other things are also important and trade-offs have to be made. It would be a strange person who chose to live in poverty when they were young in order to be wealthy in retirement, and few people are prepared to live a life of austere self-denial to minimise every health risk. Ask a person if they value health and money, they will probably say yes, but ask them if they value fun and freedom, they will also say yes. People's desires are often in conflict with one another. We genuinely want to avoid dying in a car crash, but we accept this risk in exchange for the benefits of fast, convenient transport. The mere fact that a person's (stated) preference is to be healthy does not mean that their (revealed) preference for junk food or alcohol is illegitimate.

If we judged people's desires by their behaviour – as economists do – we would not conclude that pristine health is their only goal. Even stated preferences do not imply that people prioritise a long life over all other considerations. When The Who sang 'I hope I die before I get old' in 1965 they were reflecting a stated preference for living fast and dying young that is not uncommon. A young man who leads an unhealthy or risk-taking lifestyle while claiming to have little or no interest in getting old is being consistent in his stated and revealed preferences. He may change his mind in later life, but that is not sufficient reason to view his youthful preferences as illegitimate.

In surveys of personal life goals, it is relationships with friends and family that tend to top the list, followed by the hope of having a good job, a dream home and 'being happy'. A poll of 2016's new year resolutions found that 46 per cent of those surveyed planned to 'enjoy life to the fullest'. This (admittedly vague) goal came top, beating 'live a healthier lifestyle' (41 per cent) and 'save more, spend less' (30 per cent) (Kirkham 2015).

The medium-term ambitions of teenagers and young adults include getting a degree, owning a home and getting married. Living a 'long and healthy life' featured in a global survey of millennials but nowhere in the world did it come higher than third as a life goal, and it consistently came below 'spend time with my family' and 'grow and learn new things' (Universum 2015).

Looked at from the other end of life, a survey asking older Americans about their regrets was topped by stories related to romance, family, education and careers. Money problems came fifth, cited by ten per cent of respondents, and health came seventh, cited by just six per cent of respondents (Morrison and Roese 2011). These are only crumbs of evidence, but are enough to show that people have aspirations other than health, longevity and saving for old age.

Conly makes the point that an individual's liberty is meaningless if he is not alive to exercise it. This is true up to a point, but a longer life does not imply a freer life, nor does it necessarily mean a better life. No one would claim that somebody who dies at 90 has, by definition, led a more fulfilling life than someone who dies at 80. Being alive, like being free, is ultimately only a means to an end, not an end in itself.

Doctors respect people's right not to be resuscitated if they fall into a coma and most of us respect people's right to commit suicide. Are we to assume that both these acts are always and everywhere irrational? Kingsley Amis stated it bluntly when he said that 'no pleasure is worth giving up for the sake of two more years in a geriatric home at Weston-super-Mare'. The philosopher Joel Feinberg (1971: 109) put it more delicately, writing:

> Sometimes it is more reasonable to assume a great risk for a great gain than to play it safe and forfeit a unique opportunity. Thus it is not necessarily more reasonable for a coronary patient to increase his life expectancy by living a life of quiet inactivity than to continue working hard at his career in the hope of achieving something important even at the risk of a sudden fatal heart attack at

any moment. There is no simple mathematical formula to guide one in making such decisions or for judging them 'reasonable' or 'unreasonable.'

These might be extreme examples, but they illustrate the costs and benefits people weigh up throughout their lives. The key word here is 'trade-off'. There are balances to be struck between short-term, medium-term and long-term aspirations, and it cannot be assumed that long-term aspirations are the most important. Moreover, the long-term goal of being happy could be reasonably pursued by a succession of short-term pleasures.

Conly shows that she is aware of such trade-offs. Echoing Sunstein, she says that one of her key criteria for coercive intervention is that 'the benefits have to be greater than the costs' (Conly 2013: 151). But who is to decide, and how? Conly wants to ban cigarettes but not alcohol because '*I think* that the benefits of drinking alcohol outweigh its dangers' (ibid.: 149 – emphasis added). Similarly, she does not want to ban sugary drinks, because 'people really enjoy soda' and because 'soda is sufficiently important to people that in some form it should remain available' (ibid.: 161–62). She even makes exceptions for some acutely life-threatening activities so long as people enjoy them (ibid.: 154):

> Even if death is an immediate risk, if an activity is sufficiently rewarding it may be worth it – we ski despite the danger of breaking our necks running into a tree, we drive, and so forth. It would be counterproductive to ban every dangerous activity.

When proposing a ban on trans fats on the basis of what is, to her, a slam dunk cost–benefit analysis, she says 'we have no reason to think the health risks of trans fats could be offset by enjoyment' (ibid.). This may be true – healthier substitutes for trans fats taste identical – but it raises the question of how much 'enjoyment' trans fats would have to give people for them to be 'sufficiently rewarding' and for a ban to be 'counterproductive'. If people enjoyed eating them as much as some people enjoy skiing, presumably they would be permitted, but if people only enjoyed them as much as people enjoy smoking they would be outlawed.

For Conly, the risks of sugary drinks are on the right side of the line – but only just. She says she would support their prohibition if future research confirmed a link between soda consumption and heart disease and weight gain (ibid.).[2] Could Conly ever be convinced that the benefits of a large restaurant portion 'outweigh its dangers'? What would it take for her to concede that cigarettes are 'important' to people or that smokers 'really enjoy' them? There seems to be a cost–benefit analysis going on here but there is no methodology, no clear logic. What are the criteria? It all seems so arbitrary.

Gerald Dworkin (1971: 188) makes similar unspecified trade-offs in his celebrated essay on paternalism. He supports compulsion when it comes to seat belts because 'the restriction is trivial in nature, interferes not at all with the

---

2   This is a strange benchmark. Since sugary drinks contain calories, they can obviously contribute to weight gain – and obesity can cause heart disease.

use or enjoyment of the activity, and does, I am assuming, considerably reduce a high risk of serious injury'. By contrast, he says that many 'ultra-hazardous activities', such as bull-fighting, sports-car racing and mountain-climbing, should not be prohibited because there are 'some risks – even very great ones – which a person is entitled to take with his life' (ibid.). But which ones? Climbing Everest has a death rate of one in fifteen and is significantly more dangerous than driving without a seat belt. We cannot know what goes through the minds of mountain climbers as they freeze to death on K2 (as one in five of those who attempt to reach the summit do). Perhaps some of them genuinely reflect on the fact that they are dying doing what they love best, but many of them may wish they had been restrained from attempting the climb. Dworkin says that a ban on mountain climbing 'completely prevents a person from engaging in an activity which may play an important role in his life and his conception of the person he is' (ibid.). The same could surely be said of some people who smoke tobacco, marijuana or opium.

Besides, what kind of coercive paternalist allows people to do things just because they enjoy them?! The more one reads of the paternalism literature, the more one is struck by *ad hoc* exceptions being made to supposedly universal principles. That these exemptions tend to reflect the public mood of the day only confirms Mill's fears about the tyranny of the majority. Smoking and eating dominate both *Against Autonomy* and Sunstein's *Why Nudge?* as if they were in a separate class of risky pursuits. When it comes to activities that pose an acute risk of death at a young age, such as motorcycling and mountaineering, paternalists have little to say other than that participants should, perhaps, be forced to wear a helmet. There must be a suspicion that dangerous sports get a free pass because they are seen as daring, unusual and physically demanding whereas drinking, smoking and drug taking are undemanding, common and intoxicating.

Prejudice and subjective opinion render the search for universal ends meaningless. Once it is understood that people's goals are varied and conflicting, the trivial truism that people value their health does not lead to any obvious conclusions about what the government should do about risky, self-regarding behaviours. In contrast to Mill's 'simple principle', hard paternalism involves a series of unquantifiable value judgements, leaving Mill's concerns about the limits of government unresolved.

Slippery slopes and runaway trains

The vague and ultimately subjective cost–benefit analysis that Conly invokes when she tells us which self-regarding behaviours should be banned raises concerns about a slippery slope of ever-increasing government interference. Conly herself mentions the possibility of forcing people to take exercise classes and she criticises various supposedly irrational activities, such as buying lottery tickets, which appear to be suitable targets for prohibition under her criteria. If 97 per cent of the US population live unhealthy lifestyles, as one study claims (Loprinizi et al. 2016), the scope for paternalism seems almost endless.

As an example of a slippery slope argument, here is an excerpt from a *Guardian* article in which the author – in all seriousness – proposes banning meat in NHS hospitals on the grounds that, like cigarettes, its consumption increases the risk of cancer (Seedhouse 2016):

> Meat eaters who enjoy a relaxing cigarette after dinner are prevented from doing so, apparently in their own and others' best interests, thanks to a blanket ban on smoking. But how can the NHS sensibly ban cigarettes as a known health hazard while simultaneously promoting meat? To endorse one known danger while completely banning a similar one makes no sense. Either it's OK to allow free choice or it's OK to prevent 'unhealthy behaviours', but you can't have it both ways. If you ban smoking you have to ban meat, which causes considerably more damage to animals, the environment and individuals than smoking. If you don't ban meat, then you can't ban smoking. Which is it to be?

Slippery slope arguments are, strictly speaking, logical fallacies. In principle, the same arguments for banning opium can be used to ban alcohol, but there is no reason to assume that one will inevitably follow the other. Each policy can be debated on its own terms. However, the existence of one law makes people more likely to accept a similar law based on the same logic. Conly freely accepts this when she observes that laws which 'may at first seem extreme, relative to the norm, can come to be seen as the status quo, which enables a step to what was considered extreme now appear moderate, and thus acceptable, regardless of merit' (Conly 2013: 115). Further, she notes that 'while progress from A to Z doesn't follow logically, we are, just as the paternalist maintains, far from entirely logical. Especially where concepts are imprecise, the hapless lawmaker is much more likely to go from a possibly justified policy to one that is not' (ibid.: 114–15).

Knowing that it can be persuasive to appeal to precedents, Conly does it herself in *Against Autonomy*. For example (ibid.: 47):

> Given that we allow paternalistic intervention in some cases (seat belts, prescription medicine) where we think intervention is very, very likely to make a person better off, we should allow it in other, similar cases.

Seat belt laws are mentioned a great deal by advocates of paternalism. Along with motorcycle helmet laws, they represent a widely accepted precedent (in Britain, at least) for legislation against victimless crimes. This was always the fear of liberals. When the House of Commons debated seat belt legislation in 1979, none who opposed it denied that wearing a seat belt improved safety. Their concern was that such paternalistic legislation would become a runaway train. As one MP, Ivan Lawrence, said (Hansard 1979):

> Why should anyone be forced by criminal sanction not to hurt himself? That was never, at least until the crash helmet legislation, a principle of our criminal law. Where

will it end? Why make driving without a seat belt a crime because it could save a thousand lives, when we could stop cigarette smoking by the criminal law and save 20,000 lives a year? Why not stop by making it criminal the drinking of alcohol, which would save hundreds of thousands of lives?

In response, John Horan MP argued that 'to regulate in these areas of smoking, sports, and so on, is to regulate people's pleasures and enjoyment. The Bill is really not the herald of some new era of prohibition, or something of that kind. To claim that it is is really too much' (ibid.). And yet the seat belt legislation has been cited ever since by parliamentarians seeking to justify everything from mandatory cycle helmets to water fluoridation to banning smoking in public places and private vehicles (Hansard 2004, 2006, 2014). Speaking in favour of plain packaging for tobacco products in 2015, Lord Hunt said (Hansard 2015):

There is general support for seat belts. Is that not the same issue? It is a legal activity, but we are right to place constraints on it to safeguard people from its worst effects.

The answer to this rhetorical question is, I would suggest, that it is not remotely the same issue. Lord Hunt's intention was to remind the audience that those who made libertarian arguments about the slippery slope in the past did so in opposition to laws that are now widely accepted. 'Noble Lords may remember the row about seatbelts: "Ooh, you can't have the nanny state making people wear seatbelts" ' said Lord Storey in a debate about banning smoking in cars in 2013. 'In the end we had the courage to fight for that, and we cut the number of deaths in traffic accidents considerably' (Hansard 2013). The audience is supposed to assume from this that the critics were wrong before and are wrong again, but this ignores their real objection. They did not oppose the legislation because they doubted it would 'cut the number of deaths'. They opposed it because it was a minor infringement of liberty that would probably lead to major infringements. The very fact that politicians continually cite the seat belt law as an accepted precedent for further hard paternalism shows that their concerns were well founded.[3]

Seat belt and helmet laws are important not because they are draconian encroachments on liberty – the encroachment is real but relatively minor – but because they patently breach Mill's harm principle and change public perception about the objectives of criminal law. For hard paternalists, this is all well and good. Conly believes that 'the reasons that justify the instances of paternalism we accept, such as seat belt laws, do indeed justify other interventions' (Conly 2013: 149). This would seem to make a whole range of private lifestyle choices fair game for regulation.

---

3 The other notable example of a widely adopted paternalistic law is drug prohibition, but the consequences of this policy have been so visibly disastrous that paternalists are reluctant to cite it as a precedent. Sarah Conly (2013: 121) claims that drugs were banned on the basis of the harm principle rather than for paternalistic reasons. I find this argument unconvincing but it is telling that she is eager to distance her philosophy from such a conspicuous example of failed prohibition.

Conly's own criteria for an acceptable act of coercion allow for considerable latitude. Hard paternalism can be justified, she says, if it is effective, if the benefits outweigh the costs, if there is no better way of achieving the same outcome, and if it advances people's long-term goals. Aside from the difficulty of making a cost–benefit analysis when the costs involve hard-to-measure psychological damage, it is the last of these criteria that creates the intractable problem. As discussed above, people have different and conflicting long-term goals. Conly brushes over this and simply assumes that anything that improves health or longevity is sufficient warrant for coercion.

Although Conly insists that her creed of banning things for people's own good will not create a runaway train of hyper-regulation, her inability to say where the line should be drawn leaves significant room for doubt. Like many paternalists, Conly might imagine herself as a benevolent dictator under her system of government, but what if she were not in charge? Under Mill's harm principle a ban on assaulting people cannot evolve into a ban on self-harming, even though injury could be prevented in both cases. Sunstein and Thaler's nudge theory also sets a limit on the size and scope of government intervention. There are no such limits to Conly's brand of hard paternalism. If the benefits of a law to an individual are perceived by the government to exceed the costs to the individual, it is justified under her terms. Just as the ability to set a natural limit on government power is a major strength of Mill's philosophy, Conly's inability to do likewise, aside from some optimistic assurances and wishful thinking, is a major weakness of hers.

The tyranny of the majority

Having little to say about how the government's hands should be tied, Conly ultimately appeals to common sense and democracy as limiting constraints. This would be cold comfort to John Stuart Mill, who argued in *On Liberty* that democracy was no constraint and that the masses could not be relied upon to protect liberty. Politicians are ultimately answerable to the people, and it was fear of the mob that drove Mill's desire to set a limit on government power. He regarded the average person as being 'moderate in inclinations' with 'no tastes or wishes strong enough to incline them to do anything unusual'. As a collective, he believed, this made them 'intolerant of any marked demonstration of individuality' (Mill 1987: 134).

Conly argues that 'we do not have to assume that law will do nothing but impose the prejudices of the majority on the minority' (Conly 2013: 62) and she gives examples of politicians moving ahead of public opinion, such as America's 1964 Civil Rights Act. However, it was the government that took civil rights away from black people in the first place, and there are plenty of other instances of minorities being persecuted in democratic countries. Slavery, religious intolerance and the criminalisation of homosexuality are three of many historical examples.

To her credit, Conly (2013: 64) does not deny that paternalistic policies based on the preferences of the majority will penalise minorities:

Surely, some people – the outliers Mill wanted to protect – will be prevented from doing what they truly want to do when paternalistic legislation is in place, even though most will be aided to do what they want to do.

This poses an ethical problem. Being prevented from doing what you want to do – from 'maximising your utility' – is a real human cost. So too is being prosecuted, fined and possibly imprisoned for taking part in proscribed activities. As much as paternalists might prefer to use legislation to 'send a message' or 'change norms', it is inevitable that their system will lead to people being prosecuted for committing victimless crimes.

Most people do not think it justifiable to imprison innocent men even if it leads to more guilty men being locked up. As Dworkin (1971: 188) notes, it is 'better ten men ruin themselves than one man be unjustly deprived of liberty'. Paternalists must be prepared to punish people who have not hurt anyone but themselves (and who have often not even done that). This is the uncomfortable trade-off and Conly tries to skirt around it by talking about 'institutional change' and punishing big business rather than individuals. She wants to ban the manufacture of cigarettes, rather than the consumption of them, and she wants to ban restaurants from serving large portions rather than making it illegal for individuals to eat too much. But this is to ignore the fact that it is invariably individuals who suffer from prohibition. The pharmaceutical company Bayer may have lost a little revenue from the banning of their brand of diamorphine ('heroin') but the real losers of the war on drugs have been opiate users. Anheuser-Busch lost considerable revenue when it had to turn to soft drinks after its beers were banned during Prohibition, but it was the drinking public who paid the greater price by way of organised crime and dangerous moonshine.

The reality is that hard paternalists punish people for their lifestyle choices and require a minority or even a majority of their fellow citizens to sacrifice their welfare and liberty for the good of others – even when others could achieve the same outcomes (such as not smoking, staying slim, avoiding drugs) without everybody else being forced to submit to the same laws. In the final analysis, coercive paternalists not only breach the harm principle, they actively cause harm.

5   NEO-PATERNALISM: AN ASSESSMENT

There is no doubt that cognitive biases such as over-optimism, inertia and *hyperbolic discounting* exist, and it cannot be denied that these biases affect decision-making. The insights of behavioural economics are interesting and should be taken seriously, but we should not get carried away. Only a minority of people respond to nudges in most of the randomised controlled trials cited by behavioural economists and not all of those experiments have been replicated successfully, whether in the laboratory or in the real world (van der Zee et al. 2017; Deaton and Cartwright 2016). The scenarios involved are sometimes trivial, often unrealistic, and the participants tend to get better with practice: that is, they become more 'rational' as they become more familiar with the scenario.

The nudgers can give us examples of people making suboptimal decisions after being subtly influenced, but these tend to be in situations where the stakes are low and the thinking is fast. It is more difficult to find examples of people acting against their stated preferences when the stakes are high and the options are laid out fairly. When people are given a straight choice between healthy and unhealthy foods – for example, between sugary and sugar-free drinks – millions of people continue to choose the unhealthy option. The large food servings that Conly wants to ban are not the default option in restaurants. It is always cheaper to abstain from alcohol than to drink, and nobody is opted-in to smoking; on the contrary, non-smoking is very much the default option in countries such as Britain. People have to make a conscious, costly effort to choose these behaviours.

No doubt inertia and hyperbolic discounting play a role in obesity, and there are some nudges that seem to help people make better nutritional choices (Arno and Thomas 2016), but nudging has little to offer smokers, alcoholics and couch potatoes. It is telling that the Behavioural Insights Team's most effective intervention in the field of health promotion was advising the government to leave e-cigarettes alone at a time when other countries were banning them (Halpern 2015: 188–97). Doing nothing is a perfectly respectable strategy – it would be worth having a unit in government telling politicians to do nothing on a full-time basis – but it illustrates the limited practical applications of nudge theory.

By contrast, coercive paternalism has limitless possibilities, many of them sinister. Despite claiming to be a means paternalist, Sarah Conly makes subjective judgements about the ends people should pursue, namely health, longevity and saving for old age. People's revealed preferences, as exhibited through their day-to-day behaviour, do not suggest that these are, in fact, their dominant ambitions and although they certainly feature as stated preferences in surveys, they are halfway down the list along with various competing aspirations. Conly's belief that longevity and financial security are desirable is hard to quibble with, but the implicit assumption that these goals trump other objectives is a value judgement that no one but the individual is qualified to make.

In practice, Conly dictates both the ends (e.g. longevity) and the means (e.g. banning large servings of food). She would only be a means paternalist if everybody explicitly stated that being slim, never smoking and living to extreme old age were their most important goals – and that every other consideration was subordinate to them. This is clearly not the universal will of humanity, or even a large part of it. If we accept that people have a variety of conflicting goals and a range of different preferences, the individual remains best placed to make the trade-offs.

Nudge is explicitly liberal while *Against Autonomy* is openly authoritarian. When, in *Why Nudge?*, Cass Sunstein departs from his own principles and gives his support to legal coercion, albeit of a mild variety, he introduces the same subjective judgements and raises the same fears of elitism, anti-individualism and the tyranny of the majority that plague Conly's brand of hard paternalism.

The contrast with Mill is stark. For all the millions of words that have been written about the harm principle, there is a clarity of thought in *On Liberty* that is not always to be found in the writings of the new breed of paternalists (the 'neo-paternalists'). In any given scenario involving the curtailment of personal freedom, we can usually guess what Mill would do. Despite promising a novel way of approaching regulation, neither nudge theorists nor coercive paternalists offer such a clear guide to lawmakers. If the nudgers were serious about their principles they would be calling for the repeal of hundreds of laws. If the hard paternalists were serious about their philosophy they would demand a raft of draconian laws. Instead, both factions seek out the middle ground of public opinion, saying little about anything other than smoking, obesity and personal debt, and appealing to subjective judgements about costs and benefits.

Searching for the 'true' self

Behavioural economics is not the threat to Mill's doctrine of liberty that the neo-paternalists think – or hope – it is. On the face of it, it is a bold claim to say that people routinely choose to do things that they do not want to do and yet that is the implicit premise of neo-paternalism. Both nudgers and coercive paternalists say that their aim is to help people pursue their own preferences *as judged by themselves*. So how do we know a person's true preferences? For Mill it was simple. We give him freedom and observe his actions (Mill 1987: 173):

> His voluntary choice is evidence that what he so chooses
> is desirable.

As a good economist, Mill believed that actions (revealed preferences) spoke louder than words (stated preferences). Paternalists, by contrast, tend to give stated preferences more weight and assume that behaviour which is inconsistent with certain aspirations is the result of external pressure or internal weakness. But talk is cheap and virtue is easy to signal. When asked about their goals, values and priorities in surveys, people know what the socially acceptable, high status answers are – things like keeping fit, doing charity work and looking after the environment – even if their real interests are watching television and drinking.

In *Inside the Nudge Unit*, David Halpern (2015: 139) details the results of two behavioural experiments that appear to show 'time-inconsistency', with people making different decisions in the here and now than they would make for their future selves:

> Around three-quarters of (Danish) workers chose fruit over chocolate when the prize was due to be delivered the following week, yet the majority instead chose chocolate when offered the choice at the point of delivery. Similarly, most people choose a healthy snack option over an unhealthy one for later in the day – especially if they have just eaten – but the reverse is true when asked immediately before the snack is available. The same appears to be true for other forms of consumption: most people choose a 'highbrow' movie (such as *Schindler's List*) over a 'lowbrow' one (such as *Four Weddings and a Funeral*) when deciding what to watch next week, but the reverse when thinking about the evening.

What should we conclude from this? Halpern says it shows that we are 'trapped in our present' and links it to hyperbolic discounting in which 'the further into the future a cost or benefit, the disproportionately smaller it becomes relative to immediate costs and benefits'. So it does, but it also shows something else.

People have a tendency to think – or hope – that they will have a different outlook in the future. If you have ever agreed, months in advance, to do something in which you are not very interested – such as going to a conference that is likely to be dreary – you will be familiar with this cognitive bias. Like an elephant in the distance, it seems very small when it is only a date in the diary. You think that you will be eager and ready when the day comes, but when it does you wonder why you ever agreed to it. This is a cognitive bias, but it tells us more about second-order preferences than it does about being 'trapped in the present'. You wish you were the kind of person who enjoyed going to tedious conferences, eating healthy food and watching highbrow films. You hope that in the near future you might become that person. But you are not that kind of person.

In the experiments above, the participants were given a straight choice. They did not have to pay for their food and films. There was nothing to sway them in the choice architecture, no nudging, no default option. Given that they opted for chocolate and *Sleepless in Seattle*, it would take a leap of faith to conclude that what they really wanted was celery and *The Piano*. Yes, they chose healthy food and highbrow films for their future selves, but putting something off until tomorrow is only one step removed from not doing it at all. At best, these experiments show that people know what an idealised version of themselves *ought* to do. Awkwardly, though, they also show what people really *want* to do.

The only cognitive bias that stands out in the example above is over-optimism about future events. It cannot seriously be claimed that people are addicted to lowbrow films. Watching them creates no health risks in the future that might be discounted by a reckless viewer. People really do prefer them, even if they know they should not. If 'true' preferences are revealed in these experiments, it is for guilty pleasures.

Second-order preferences, otherwise known as 'preferred preferences', are not enough to base a system of coercion around. For example, I would like to be able to play the piano. If I took lessons and practised for an hour a day, I would presumably become a fairly competent pianist within a few years. It would involve a sacrifice of time and money but it would allow me to fulfil an aspiration. The trouble is that there are other things I want to do with my time, some of which might not provide the long-term satisfaction of being a proficient piano player – how would I know? – but I do them anyway because I like them.

Perhaps I am making the wrong choice by failing to take piano lessons. Perhaps I would be an objectively better person if I was a pianist. Certainly, I am not lying when I say that I would like to be able to play the piano. So should the government cajole me into taking piano lessons? Should it discourage me from doing the things I do instead? Or should it accept that playing the piano is only one of many aspirations and that I would do it if I really wanted to?

The reality is that playing the piano is my second-order preference. When I say 'I want to play the piano', what I really mean is that 'I want to be the kind of person who can be bothered to learn to play the piano'. But I am obviously *not* that kind of person otherwise I would have done it already.

Conly touches on second-order preferences in her discussion of smoking. She writes that 'while people want cigarettes, they generally want not to want them' (Conly 2013: 177). In other words, they want to be the kind of people who don't want to smoke; the kind of people who get no benefit from nicotine. And yet they are not. Some would say that their sovereignty has been undermined by the addictive qualities of nicotine – an issue we shall return to in a later chapter – but people claim to want to do all sorts of things that they are not being prevented from doing. They say they want to get a new job or a new partner. They claim to want to move to another country. None of these aspirations require insurmountable effort and some people achieve them, just as some people quit smoking and lose weight. As Jacob Sullum says of those who claim to want to emigrate in his book *For Your Own Good*: 'The fact that these people stay where they are does not mean they are powerless to change their situations. Rather, it indicates the benefits they would have to give up' (Sullum 1998: 246).

Stated preferences give individuals a pain-free way of fantasising about future benefits without paying the costs, while second-order preferences allow people to imagine enjoying the things they hate and disliking the things they love. Economists are right to dismiss such sentiments and focus on what people actually do in the real world. It is absurd to pretend that the idealised self is the real person or that people can be remoulded as their higher selves through government intervention.

Conly says that 'the goal of paternalistic legislation is to allow us to be more like ourselves' (Conly 2013: 88). But which self? She does not mean us, the flesh and blood human beings reading her book. She means the people she imagines we would want to be if we were more 'rational'. But to the paternalist, 'rational' is a euphemism for their own tastes, prejudices and desires, giving the illusion of objectivity to fundamentally subjective preferences. The desire to make people 'more like themselves' is, more often than not, a desire to make people more like the paternalist. Isaiah Berlin (1969: 133) described this well in 'Two Concepts of Liberty' when, ventriloquising dictatorial paternalists through the ages, he wrote:

> I may declare that [people] are actually aiming at what in their benighted state they consciously resist, because there exists within them an occult entity – their latent rational will, or their 'true' purpose – and that this entity, although it is belied by all that they overtly feel and do and say, is their 'real' self, of which the poor empirical self in space and time may know nothing or little; and that this inner spirit is the only self that deserves to have its wishes taken into account. Once I take this view, I am in a position to ignore the actual wishes of men or societies, to bully, oppress, torture them in the name, and on behalf, of their 'real' selves in the secure knowledge that

> whatever is the true goal of man (happiness, performance
> of duty, wisdom, a just society, self-fulfilment) must be
> identical with his freedom – the free choice of his 'true',
> albeit often submerged and inarticulate, self.

Sarah Conly appeals to the insights of behavioural economics, but she does not claim that people eat too much
or smoke because they are unable to stop themselves or
are ignorant of the risks. Her reason for wanting to use
coercion is more straightforward. She thinks people who
choose to eat too much and smoke are simply wrong and,
after 180 pages of philosophical justification, she says so
explicitly (Conly 2013: 179–80):

> The reason for intervention is that we don't trust you
> to choose rightly. We are taking away freedom in these
> cases because we don't think people will choose well
> themselves. We don't think preserving your autonomy,
> your freedom to act based on your own decision, is worth
> the costs, in part because your decision making is done
> so badly that your freedom is used very poorly.

Elsewhere in her book, Conly denies that her agenda is
elitist but, as this quote suggests, coercive paternalism is
not a collective effort in which every member of society
recognises their shared fallibility and asks for a benevolent
government to restrain them for their own good. It is the
judgement of one group being imposed on another.

The hypothesis that vast numbers of people act against
their interests so often and for so long as a result of

ignorance or irrationality requires extraordinary evidence; evidence that has never been presented. A more compelling hypothesis is presented by mainstream economics, namely that individuals value health and are cognisant of risk but make trade-offs between the two because longevity does not trump all their other life goals. The individual may not be perfectly rational or perfectly informed but, assuming he is an adult of sound mind, his actions are a better guide to his preferences than any theory based on the presumption that he spends his whole life, or a large part of it, in a false consciousness doing the exact opposite of what he intends.

6 'PUBLIC HEALTH' PATERNALISM

When Mill offered examples of illiberal laws in *On Liberty* he focused mostly on religion. The Sabbatarian movement's campaign against Sunday recreations was then at the height of its success and Mill condemned the Puritans' campaign to suppress 'all public, and nearly all private, amusements' (Mill 1987: 154). But of all the 'gross usurpations upon the liberty of private life' Mill identified in his own day, it was prohibition of alcohol in the US state of Maine and the UK Alliance's efforts to introduce the same law to Britain that drew his sharpest barbs (ibid.: 156). The Alliance, whose full name was the United Kingdom Alliance for the Suppression of the Traffic in All Intoxicating Liquors, raised Mill's hackles by using a warped version of the harm principle to justify their attack on alcohol. A spokesman for the group claimed that other people's drinking violated his 'social rights' because it 'impedes my right to free moral and intellectual development by surrounding my path with dangers and by weakening and demoralising society' (ibid.: 158). Mill called this a 'monstrous' principle which, in practice, 'acknowledges no right to any freedom whatever, except perhaps to that of holding opinions in secret' (ibid.).

Mill also criticised the use of licensing laws to restrict the availability of alcohol, a policy he believed was 'suited only to a state of society in which the labouring classes are avowedly treated as children and savages' (ibid.: 172). He did not object to licensing laws *per se*, nor did he disapprove of taxing alcohol as a luxury. It was the paternalistic intent he found objectionable. Taxing drink and drugs with the specific aim of reducing demand was, he said, 'a measure differing only in degree from their entire prohibition' (ibid.: 170).

In the nineteenth century it was drinking, rather than smoking and obesity, that health paternalists focused their attention on, so Mill naturally wrote more about alcohol than he did about tobacco or food. The only mention of smoking in *On Liberty* comes when Mill lists activities that are so commonplace that they are under no threat of suppression.[1] He was, of course, writing long before the health risks of cigarette smoking were adequately understood – indeed, long before cigarette smoking became popular – but nothing in *On Liberty* suggests that he would have applied different rules to tobacco than he did to alcohol or opium, which is to say that he would have opposed any paternalistic measure designed to deter its use.

Aside from a few remnants of the Victorian age, such as Sunday trading laws, religion plays little part in British paternalism today. For the most part, blasphemy, cursing

---

1   He writes that 'a person may, without blame, either like or dislike rowing, or smoking, or music, or athletic exercises, or chess, or cards, or study, because both those who like each of these things and those who dislike them are too numerous to be put down' (Mill 1987: 133).

and most forms of sexual deviancy are tolerated both in law and by society. Once viewed as fitting targets for government compulsion, these issues have become matters of private conscience.

Attitudes towards health, meanwhile, have gone in the opposite direction. Several writers have commented on the similarities between the modern health movement and old time religion, with their shared preoccupation with 'drugs, tobacco smoking, overeating (gluttony), consumption of alcohol, drinking of caffeine-containing beverages, and sexual license' (Edgley and Brissett 1990: 260). Lifestyle decisions that were once regarded as private matters have become issues of public concern and it is under the banner of 'public health' that paternalism breaks new ground. In *Against Autonomy*, Sarah Conly notes approvingly that 'the field of public health has been one of the few to systematically suggest interventions in behaviour' (Conly 2013: 152). With the exception of her concerns about financial security, all of her examples involve smoking or obesity. In *Why Nudge?*, Cass Sunstein's main examples of new, harder nudges are graphic warnings and retail display bans for tobacco products. In Julian Le Grand and Bill New's book *Government Paternalism*, the big idea is smoking licences.

The paternalist's gaze has turned decisively towards the health of individuals.

The logic of 'public health'

Although the 'public health' lobby borrows ideas and rhetoric from both hard and soft paternalists, it is distinct from them by virtue of being a political movement rather than a philosophy. 'Public health' paternalists are essentially a single-issue pressure group, a subset of 'ends paternalists' who believe, as Sunstein (2014a: 62) notes, 'that longevity is what is most important'. This puts them in the same bracket as Sarah Conly even if, like Conly, they think of themselves as 'means paternalists' helping people to achieve goals that they have set for themselves.

Like Conly, they give short shrift to nudge paternalism, and for the same reason (Marteau et al. 2011; Bonnell et al. 2011). A report on public health ethics by the Nuffield Council explains that in many instances 'libertarian paternalism is not suitable as it may allow too much choice' (Nuffield Council on Bioethics 2007: 25). They are open to using nudge-style tactics in the first instance but if they fail to bring about sufficient behavioural change then 'a more invasive public policy may be needed' (ibid.: 23). To illustrate the chasm between libertarian paternalists and 'public health' paternalists, consider the Nuffield Council's proposed 'nudge' of banning cigarettes from sale unless they are 'non-addictive and do not cause harm to health' – in effect, full prohibition – but with an exemption that would allow cigarettes to be sold 'only through channels such as mail ordering or similar, where more effort needs to be put into [buying them]'. It is highly debatable whether this counts as a nudge since Thaler and Sunstein (2008: 6) explicitly state that if people want to smoke cigarettes, they will 'not force them to do otherwise – or even make things hard for them', but this hardly matters since the Nuffield Council rejected the idea on the grounds that 'the possibility of opting out is too risky' (ibid.: 24). In other words, if you permit consenting adults to buy cigarettes by mail order, some of them will do so.

In their day-to-day political activities, 'public health' paternalists rarely attempt to justify their position on ethical grounds, preferring instead to talk about 'evidence-based policy' (see Whyte 2013). This keeps the conversation on the consequentialist turf of 'does it work?' rather than opening up the question 'is it right?', but their consequentialism is of a narrow sort. If a policy is believed to prolong life or curtail risky behaviour, then it 'works' and becomes 'evidence-based' *per se*. Other consequences are largely ignored, including the implications for people's welfare, unless they directly affect health.

'Public health' paternalism is quasi-utilitarian in the sense that it uses regulation to increase aggregate longevity and reduce aggregate health risks. If utilitarianism is about the greatest happiness for the greatest number, then 'public health' paternalism is about the greatest health for the greatest number. Gostin and Gostin (2009: 217) claim that 'Public health paternalism is concerned primarily with overall societal welfare'. It is not. It is concerned with one aspect of societal welfare which the paternalist thinks is more important than other aspects. As Carl Phillips notes, it does not fit within any recognised framework of welfare economics and is a 'pseudo-ethic' (Phillips 2016a):

> It is not welfarist, because the measure is not welfare, but merely one arbitrarily-chosen component of welfare,

reduction of disease. No one tries to defend this goal by claiming that if it were adopted as an ethic it would make the world a better place. It clearly would not do so. It certainly does not reflect the empirical reality of how anyone chooses to live their life.

In an article advocating the prohibition of cigarettes, Grill and Voigt (2015: 2–3) assert that 'more life is better' and 'more freedom is not always better'. As a short summary of the 'public health' worldview, this double whammy of bald assertions is tough to beat. Both statements are plainly subjective judgements. A libertarian might argue the exact opposite. Others would take the middle ground depending on circumstances. Contrary to Gostin and Gostin (2009), there is no guarantee that efforts to improve the health of the population will improve *societal welfare*. On the contrary, 'public health' policies which raise the costs and reduce the benefits of people's first choice preferences are likely to damage their welfare and therefore damage the welfare of society as a whole.

Policies which interfere in consumer choice to advance one component of welfare cannot be justified on utilitarian grounds, nor can they be justified on liberal grounds. Some 'public health' policies can be defended on economic grounds, such as addressing negative externalities, even if their primary intention is to change behaviour for paternalistic reasons. But 'public health' paternalism cannot be justified by welfare economics or utilitarianism. It is simply a form of ends paternalism in which health and longevity are assumed to be overriding goals.

Public health versus 'public health'

The case for government action on public health issues is strongest when there is a threat to health that can only be countered by collective action. Collective action does not necessarily mean government action, but if the term 'public health' meant anything in Mill's day, it meant tackling health risks in the shared environment which cannot be controlled by the individual, such as air pollution, or those involving people (or animals) who carry infectious diseases. Factories pumping coal smoke into a congested city and travellers coming home with Ebola pose a clear risk of unavoidable harm to others and are therefore a potential justification for coercion under the harm principle. It is not the scale of the risk nor the number of people affected that turns a health problem into a public health problem. It is the lack of consent from those who are put at risk and their inability to reduce the risk without collective action.

Since the 1970s, however, the scope of public health action has moved beyond hygiene and contagious disease to target self-regarding personal behaviour. As Richard A. Epstein (2004: 1421) explains, the modern 'public health' movement 'treats any health issue as one of public health so long as it affects large numbers of individuals'. This has led to a focus on personal habits which are risk factors for non-communicable diseases, such as heart disease, diabetes and cancer. 'Our public health problems are not, strictly speaking, public health questions at all', write Gostin and Gostin (2009: 220). 'They are questions of individual lifestyle'. In this view, 'public health' is the aggregated private health outcomes of the nation, and prevention involves modifying any factors that influence them.[2]

Social reformers have been using legislation to clean up the environment since the nineteenth century, but the use of laws to regulate lifestyles opens up 'a whole new way of operating for public health' (Berridge 2016: 71). Obesity is now routinely described as a 'public health epidemic' despite being neither contagious nor a disease. Smoking, drinking and even gambling have been brought under the umbrella of 'public health' and are also referred to as 'epidemics' despite having such long histories that they are the very opposite; they are endemic. An epidemic of non-communicable disease is an oxymoron, but the use of such terms encourages the public to tolerate the same level of state intervention in matters of lifestyle as they would if they were in the midst of a viral outbreak. As Epstein (2004: 1462) notes, 'designating obesity as a public health epidemic is designed to signal that state coercion is appropriate when it is not.'

In an article arguing that there is no moral difference between restricting food advertising and evacuating people from the site of a nuclear accident, Herington et al. (2014: 27) acknowledge that it is largely a question of using the most persuasive rhetoric:

> To counteract the liberty-oriented position, those who favour a more interventionist role for the state have recently

---

2   To distinguish between the traditional and contemporary public health movements I will put speech marks around 'public health' when referring to the modern movement that focuses on private, non-collective health risks.

argued for labelling obesity as a public health emergency. In this view, while we might accept that the state should ordinarily refrain from interfering with the self-regarding behaviour of its citizens, that presumption is much less stringent during a public health emergency. By labelling obesity as a public health emergency, policy-makers could override concerns about individual liberty in order to pursue more interventionist policies designed to guide consumer choices toward healthier lifestyles.

Since obesity is a slow-growing and reversible risk factor for some chronic diseases of old age, the authors of this article have to resort to extraordinarily creative arguments to redefine terms such as 'emergency' and 'imminent harm' to make them fit their purpose while attributing beliefs to John Stuart Mill that he surely did not hold. Like other 'public health' paternalists, they maintain that an individual health risk becomes a matter for the government when many people are involved and when the government could do something about it. The activities in question do not *have* to be addressed by collective action – indeed, individual action is often more effective – but because they *can* be addressed by collective action that is enough to make them suitable targets for government intervention.

This widens the scope enormously because almost anything *can* be affected by government intervention and almost anything *can* affect the health of individuals. As Rothstein (2009: 86) notes, any list of 'root causes' or 'social determinants' of poor health must include 'war, famine, crime, poverty, unemployment, income inequality, environmental degradation, lack of economic development, human rights violations, poor education, inadequate housing, lack of natural resources and unresponsive governments.' Some 'public health' groups believe that their mission does indeed encompass all of these issues and more but, as Rothstein argues, there is no reason to think that redefining social and economic problems as 'public health issues' makes them any easier to solve. Given that public health officials have limited resources, coercive powers and no democratic mandate, it makes sense for them to focus on controlling contagious diseases rather than embroiling themselves in complex and controversial political issues which are beyond their immediate field of expertise.

Consent

'Public health' paternalists do not necessarily see themselves as part of a paternalistic tradition. Rather, they see themselves as an outpost of the medical community; they proscribe while doctors prescribe. But there is a crucial difference between a 'public health' activist and a medical practitioner. While medics require the consent of the patient, 'public health' professionals do not ask for consent and their interventions often contradict the wishes of the people they are 'treating'. This is a serious ethical problem. As Charlton (1995: 609) says: 'Good intentions are not enough when it comes to imposing interventions upon an unconsenting population.'

Some paternalists have argued that no government policy has the consent of every individual and so there is no need to expect it in the case of 'public health' policies (Wilson 2011). While it is true that the government does not ask every individual for permission to run the army or build an airport, these are functions that ineluctably require collective action. When public goods are at stake and one size has to fit all, majoritarian democracy is the least bad system. A minority will always be unsatisfied with the course of action, and that is unfortunate, but when a nation is required to choose a single path it is unavoidable. Only one view can prevail.

But the mere fact that governments do not require consent when making decisions that have to be made collectively does not justify governments bypassing consent when it comes to decisions that individuals can make for themselves. Health is not a public good. People cannot avoid air pollution by setting their own rules, but they can control their intake of sugary drinks. This is a fundamental distinction. When it comes to personal lifestyle decisions, collective action is unnecessary. Everybody can get their own way.

Much of the 'public health' literature treats the shift from preventing contagious diseases to regulating private behaviour as an inevitable consequence of communicable diseases being largely eradicated in developed countries. With communicable diseases vanquished, they say, non-communicable diseases took their place and became the new challenge for public health officials to fight. And since lifestyle factors are associated with non-communicable diseases, it is only natural that public health campaigners regulate lifestyles.

I would argue that it is neither natural nor inevitable. The natural conclusion to a successful campaign is stopping. A movement which succeeds in ending a contagious disease might be expected to leave enough resources in place to prevent further outbreaks but otherwise disband. Instead, the public health lobby has shifted its attention to policing the self-regarding behaviour of individuals, most of whom are dying in their eighth decade or beyond and who are not asking for their help. This is not so much mission creep as mission leap. The new 'public health' movement has taken on a fundamentally different objective and, in so doing, 'has embraced measures that go far beyond the very limited recognition of justifiable paternalism in conventional bioethical accounts' (Bayer and Fairchild 2004: 491).

When 'public health' paternalists claim that they are merely continuing long-standing, uncontroversial public health work it seems to be more of an attempt to rebut the accusation that they are part of a 'nanny state' than to provide a robust ethic for their actions. For example, in his article 'The Ethics of Smoking', Robert E. Goodin (1989: 587) appeals to public health precedents:

> We do not leave it to the discretion of consumers, however well informed, whether or not to drink grossly polluted water, ingest grossly contaminated foods, or inject grossly dangerous drugs. We simply prohibit such things on grounds of public health...

Goodin argues that a ban on the sale of tobacco, or even a ban on smoking itself, could be justified on similar grounds. At the very least, he seems to be exposing the intellectual inconsistency of libertarians who object to some prohibitions on self-regarding behaviour while ignoring others.

His analogy does not hold, however. It is not against the law to drink polluted water or eat contaminated food. It is against the law to *sell* them, but that is an issue of consumer protection rather than health paternalism. Since nobody would wish to buy 'grossly contaminated food', the only way it could be sold would be to pass it off as uncontaminated food – in other words, to sell it fraudulently. A ban on selling rotten meat is, in practice, a ban on unscrupulous butchers conning their customers. It is not a question of preventing well-informed consumers satisfying their appetite for contaminated food. If people genuinely wanted to buy rotten meat, libertarians would not stand in their way, just as they do not stand in the way of those who make the informed decision to buy unpasteurised milk, tobacco or, indeed, 'grossly dangerous drugs'.[3]

A ban on drinking polluted water and eating rotten meat would be so unnecessary that it is scarcely worth observing that it would also be illiberal. There is no demand for these activities because they confer no benefits. By contrast, there is significant demand for tobacco because it does confer benefits. The comparison is specious.

---

3   Most of which have been made grossly dangerous by their prohibition.

Risk

'Public health' paternalists have a peculiar tendency to view the population as something other than the sum of the individuals in it. Consequently, they make statements like this (Gostin and Gostin 2009: 217):

> Public health paternalism is concerned primarily with overall societal welfare rather than individual preferences. It is intended to benefit the community as a whole rather than any given person. It purports to save statistical, rather than individual, lives. Its goal is not to affect personal choices, but to build a healthier population. Government's responsibility is to the collective, as well as the individual, so it may be just as important to safeguard the population from chronic disease as infectious disease.

To anyone who is not familiar with the 'public health' movement, these ideas are close to gibberish. The last sentence is a non sequitur and the reader might wonder why 'individual preferences' are antithetical to 'overall societal welfare'. How can a community benefit if the individuals within it do not? And, most perplexingly, how can a statistical life be saved without an individual's life being saved?

The answer seems to be that different rules apply when individuals are brought together in large numbers and described as a population (ibid.: 218):

> Seen from an individual's perspective, it is hard to refute Mill's argument that there are 'good reasons for

remonstrating with him, or reasoning with him, or persuading him, or entreating him, but not for compelling him or visiting him with any evil in case he do otherwise'. However, seen from the population perspective, moving the activities of millions of people in the direction of behaviours guided by rigorous science will almost certainly improve overall health. A population that smokes less, drinks in moderation, eats well and exercises will have improved health and longevity.

This, again, is a non sequitur. The authors appear to agree that it would be wrong to coerce an individual into smoking less, drinking less, eating well and exercising, but approve of coercion if millions of people are dealt with simultaneously. This makes no sense. If it is acceptable to do something to millions of people, it must be acceptable to do it to one. Conversely, if it is unacceptable to do something to one person it must be unacceptable – worse, even – to do it to millions. The justification that population-wide measures would 'improve overall health' is irrelevant to Mill's argument about self-ownership.

The focus on aggregate statistics from large populations serves to distance the paternalist from the realities of individual's lives. Millions of complex personal trade-offs are reduced to a scary-sounding number of preventable deaths. Risk at the personal level becomes certainty at the population level. While the individual engages in a risky activity knowing that there is only a chance of being harmed by it and that death can only be postponed, never prevented (and, if he is statistically literate, that reducing risk from one disease necessarily increases the risk of other diseases), the 'public health' paternalist looks over the whole population and knows with certainty that *someone* will be killed by it. Individuals deal with risk, which can be tolerated, while 'public health' paternalists can look over the whole globe and find large numbers of lives being lost to some avoidable activity or other.

If the population is big enough and the time-frame long enough, even small risks can be blamed for a substantial death toll. For example, oropharyngeal cancer is a relatively uncommon form of cancer which kills around 2,000 people in Britain each year. According to epidemiological research, 5,000 new cases of oropharyngeal cancer are attributable to light drinking worldwide each year (Bagnardi et al. 2013). The same research suggests that light drinking is also responsible for 5,000 cases of breast cancer worldwide. When this study was released to the press in 2012, one of its authors told women to 'moderate [their drinking] or avoid it altogether' because it 'is a relevant public health issue' (Borland 2012).

But is it? 10,000 cases in a world of seven billion people suggests that the risk to the individual is rather small. The epidemiological research found that light drinking was associated with an increased risk from oropharyngeal cancer of 17 per cent. This means that light drinking increases a person's lifetime risk of developing oropharyngeal cancer from a small fraction of 1 per cent to a slightly larger fraction of 1 per cent. Breast cancer is much more common, affecting one in eight British women and yet the increased risk from light drinking is just 5 per cent, thereby turning an absolute lifetime risk of around 12.5 per cent into a lifetime risk of around 13 per cent. To the individual, these are little more than rounding errors. Few, if any, of us would sacrifice the pleasure of drinking alcohol in response to such a negligible health risk. It is for that reason that paternalists prefer to give us big numbers ('10,000 deaths a year') or relative risks ('17 per cent more likely') than to tell us the absolute risk.[4] Binge drinking may increase our risk of liver cirrhosis sixfold but, as Allmark (2006: 4) notes, this statistic is 'virtually useless for rational decision-making' unless we know what our odds of getting liver cirrhosis are to begin with (about 1 in 5,000 in any given year, in case you're wondering).

The 'public health' paternalist does not concern himself with odds, trade-offs or the size of the risk to the individual. When looking at mortality statistics he does not concern himself with the age at which people succumb to their 'lifestyle-related diseases', nor does he see what disease would have affected them had they avoided the avoidable disease. All he sees are the thousands of preventable deaths somewhere in the world that make light drinking 'a relevant public health issue'.

I could cite larger risks than those associated with light drinking – risks big enough not to need multiplying by the population of the whole planet to make an impact – but that would not alter the basic point that a risk that is tolerable to an individual cannot be intolerable to a population.

---

4 Public health bodies occasionally stress absolute risks but only when they are trying to ease concerns about cancer-causing agents that are not on their hit list, such as X-rays and hormone replacement therapy.

Neither the size of the risk nor the number of people who engage in the activity make the intervention any more (or less) ethical.

In summary, none of the arguments made to justify the 'public health' movement *as a form of paternalism* stand up. It is not a form of means paternalism, as some claim, because nobody in the real world shares its implicit assumption that minimising health risks to an extreme degree is an overriding life goal. Nor can the modern version of public health be seen as a legitimate and natural extension of the battle against infectious disease, because the need for collective action simply does not exist when health outcomes are determined by self-regarding behaviour.

7 THE POLITICS OF 'PUBLIC HEALTH' PATERNALISM

Being a political movement, the literature of 'public health' paternalism differs from that of the academic texts discussed in earlier chapters in two important respects. Firstly, it tends to focus on short-term policy objectives rather than present a full vision of what it thinks society should look like. Long-term objectives are rarely made public, perhaps because the logical outcomes are so extreme that they would alarm the median voter. Only recently, for example, has the goal of cigarette prohibition been openly discussed in the 'public health' literature despite it being the only natural conclusion of the anti-smoking crusade (Grill and Voigt 2015).

Secondly, in their eagerness to secure policy goals, 'public health' paternalists are reluctant to acknowledge costs. Sunstein talks freely about the 'psychic costs' that can be suffered by those who are subjected to hard paternalism and Conly accepts that some people will be similarly disadvantaged. By contrast, 'public health' paternalists rarely acknowledge that their policies have victims. By denying or ignoring the private benefits individuals receive from the consumption of tobacco, alcohol and 'junk food', they bypass the need for cost–benefit analyses. If there are no costs incurred by suppressing these habits, suppression can only be positive. Even the most obvious economic consequences of their policies, such as the regressive impact of sin taxes or the damage done by smoking bans to the hospitality industry, are countered with denial and sophistry. For political reasons, 'public health' policies must be presented as win–wins.

Some of the arguments and assumptions of 'public health' paternalists have already been discussed in the chapter about coercive paternalism, but there are others which are either unique to this strand of paternalism or put a new spin on older arguments. Each of them seeks to justify government intervention in self-regarding behaviour without rejecting mainstream economics outright. Indeed, such is the attachment to the harm principle in liberal democracies that 'public health' paternalists feel compelled to invoke it even as they narrow the definition of voluntary, self-regarding actions to such an extent that all actions become other-regarding and non-voluntary (and therefore suitable targets for government intervention). With a nod to Mill, they argue that they are protecting individuals from harm committed by commercial interests, and with a nod to mainstream economics they argue that unhealthy personal behaviour is substantially non-voluntary and caused by market failures.

Industry as an agent of harm

In a society in which it is broadly accepted that people may do harm to themselves but not to others, the self-regarding nature of health issues such as obesity is a major hurdle for those who want to intervene in people's lifestyles. From whom does the gluttonous couch potato need protecting if not from himself? The answer, say 'public health' paternalists, is the food industry. By switching attention from the buyer to the seller, they portray the individual as victim and the industry as aggressor. And since society tolerates a higher degree of regulation for companies than it does for individuals, legislation that is paternalistic in intent can be presented as protecting consumers from injuries inflicted by companies.

To take a typical example, an Australian professor of public health has written about the 'ubiquitous availability, accessibility, advertising and promotion of junk foods that exploit people's vulnerabilities'. Given this supposedly predatory behaviour by big business, she argues that it is 'important not to blame victims for responding as expected to unhealthy food environments' (Lee 2016).

Since advertising and promotion are much the same thing, and accessibility is the same as availability, it appears that the crimes of the food industry in this instance amount to putting products on the shelves and telling people about them. To suggest that people are 'victims' because they have been given options and information is undiluted paternalism; it treats adults like children.

In a similar vein, another proponent of the new model of 'public health', Lindsay Wiley (2012: 269), also portrays availability and advertising as forms of coercion:

There is no meaningful consent to the overrepresentation of fast food outlets and underrepresentation of full service grocery stores in low-income neighbourhoods. There is no meaningful consent to exposure to advertising on the sides of city busses extolling the virtues of dollar-menu cheeseburgers.

There is no acknowledgement here of the laws of supply and demand. If the grocery stores were overflowing with customers while fast food restaurants stood empty, there would be more of the former and fewer of latter. People do not 'consent', in a political sense, to outlets opening up, but their patronage is its own endorsement. People do not consent to advertisements being put up either, but they are free to ignore them. Neither availability nor advertising are remotely coercive. By contrast, the 'public health' response of banning advertising and denying planning permission to fast food outlets requires the full force of law.

The notion that preventing the sale of a product is a means of preventing harm to others is given short shrift in the wider literature on paternalism. Dworkin (1971: 183) dismissed it in his classic essay of 1971:

> Thus we might ban cigarette manufacturers from continuing to manufacture their product on the grounds that we are preventing them from causing illness to others in the same way that we prevent other manufacturers from releasing pollutants into the atmosphere, thereby causing danger to the members of the community. The difference is, however, that in the former but not the latter case the harm is of such a nature that it could be avoided by those individuals affected if they so chose. The incurring

of the harm requires, so to speak, the active cooperation of the victim. It would be mistaken theoretically and hypocritical in practice to assert that our interference in such cases is just like our interference in standard cases of protecting others from harm.

John Stuart Mill accepted the need for product regulation to protect the public from unseen danger but made an explicit distinction between regulations which protect people from others and those which protect people from themselves (Mill 1987: 164–65):

As the principle of individual liberty is not involved in the doctrine of free trade, so neither is it in most of the questions which arise respecting the limits of that doctrine, as, for example, what amount of public control is admissible for the prevention of fraud by adulteration; how far sanitary precautions, or arrangements to protect workpeople employed in dangerous occupations, should be enforced on employers. Such questions involve considerations of liberty only in so far as leaving people to themselves is always better, *caeteris paribus*, than controlling them; but that they may be legitimately controlled for these ends is in principle undeniable. On the other hand, there are questions relating to interference with trade which are essentially questions of liberty, such as the Maine Law [which banned the sale of alcohol], already touched upon; the prohibition of the importation of opium into China; the restriction of the sale of poisons – all cases, in short, where the object of the interference is to make it impossible or difficult to obtain a particular commodity. These interferences are objectionable, not as infringements on the liberty of the producer or seller, but on that of the buyer.

The right to buy is indivisible from the right to sell, just as the right to be informed is indivisible from the right to inform. It is impossible to violate the right of industry to sell a product without violating the right of the individual to buy it. Big Tobacco, Big Food, Big Alcohol and Big Soda are lined up as bogeymen but it is usually consumers, not executives, who bear the brunt of taxes, bans and restrictions. As Christopher Hitchens remarked in 1994, 'naive indignation about the tobacco industry is no more than a populist decoration for a campaign that actually targets the consumers rather than the producers' (Hitchens 2011: 284).

From the perspective of paternalists, the advantage of attacking the paper tigers of industry is that it appeals to the many people who are distrustful of big business, if not of capitalism in general, and it allows them to claim that they are not infringing the rights of individuals, merely regulating corporations. Although it is quite possible to regulate a product without infringing on the freedom of consumers, the kind of regulation envisaged by 'public health' paternalists goes far beyond consumer protection. An article written by three 'public health' academics entitled 'E-cigarettes should be regulated' concludes that the sale of nicotine fluid for e-cigarettes should be illegal. This, surely, is a rather extreme definition of 'regulated' (McKee et al. 2016).

Bans on the promotion and sale of certain products are frequently discussed as if they were mere restrictions on corporations. For example, when Michael Bloomberg, then the mayor of the New York City, proposed banning the sale of sugary drinks in sizes larger than 473 ml, a supporter framed the policy in terms of soft drink companies demanding the 'right to sell non-nutritional substances to young people' (Holpuch 2012). But the real question is whether people – young or old – should have the right to *buy* 'non-nutritional substances'.[1] One can argue that they do not, but this requires an explicitly paternalistic outlook and a better moral justification than merely claiming that individuals need protection from commercial enterprises.

Negative externalities

If anti-industry sentiments are better viewed as rhetoric than serious arguments, 'public health' paternalists invoke some more credible arguments about market failure which merit discussion. Each of them raises legitimate concerns that could justify some form of government action and yet in each case the 'solution' goes far beyond what is necessary to improve the market. In the end, it makes the market more dysfunctional.

A colloquial summary of Mill's harm principle is that your right to swing your fist ends at my nose. A punch on the nose is a negative externality and can justify government

---

1   Aside from the fact that sugary drinks are not 'non-nutritional' (sugar is a nutrient), it is characteristic of 'public health' campaigners to focus on sales to young people when pushing for bans that will affect everyone.

intervention. Similarly, there are externalities associated with smoking and drinking. A dropped cigarette can cause a fire. A drunk can start a fight. Second-hand smoke and rowdy behaviour can be a nuisance.

None of these side effects are inherent to alcohol and tobacco *per se*. Rather, they stem from the behaviour of the user. Since most people drink alcohol without becoming violent and most smokers extinguish their cigarettes safely, it is an open question how much we should blame a product for its misuse. Violence, criminal damage and disturbing the peace are illegal regardless of the circumstances and so the case for clamping down on alcohol as a specific cause rests on the likelihood that excessive drinking will lead to more incidents. Nevertheless, it cannot be denied that alcohol-related violence would not exist without alcohol, and cigarette-related fires would not exist without cigarettes.

The preferred response of economists to such externalities is to shift the costs from the third party to the user with a Pigouvian tax. It is assumed that the socially optimal level of consumption will be reached when the price of the product reflects not only the benefits enjoyed by the consumer but also the costs inflicted on other people. It is a neat idea in theory although it becomes more complicated in practice because 'costs' can be defined as broadly as the economist wishes them to be.

'Public health' paternalists support taxation of unhealthy products but for a different reason: higher prices generally lead to lower rates of consumption. Those who seek a 'tobacco free world' (*Lancet* 2015) evidently believe that the optimal level of tobacco consumption is zero. Those who campaign against alcohol and sugary drinks are rarely so explicitly abolitionist, but their aim is always to drive down consumption.[2] Raising taxes is one way of achieving this and Arthur Pigou appears to offer a non-paternalistic economic justification for doing so.

The perception that drinkers, smokers and the obese impose significant costs on others appears to validate 'sin taxes' and, in Britain, the 'cost to the NHS' argument is perhaps the most intuitively persuasive justification for lifestyle regulation. In a healthcare system funded by involuntary contributions, one person has to pay for another person's healthcare. This is an 'induced externality' because state intervention has laid the foundations for externalities to thrive, thereby creating demand for further state intervention (Wiley et al. 2013: 89). If the government compels citizens to pay for one another's education, healthcare, pensions and welfare benefits, there will always be someone who can complain that somebody else has made them worse off.

It is naive to assume that a reduction in unhealthy behaviour will result in tax cuts for the public. For example, dramatic declines in rates of tooth decay and heart disease have not reduced the number of dentists and heart surgeons (Rose 2008: 37). Nevertheless, collectively funded public services foster resentment towards those who are

---

2   Prohibitionists have sought an alcohol-free world in the past (Snowdon 2011: 71–98) and the UK's Chief Medical Officer claims that there is 'no safe level of drinking'. Campaigners in New Zealand explicitly seek a 'sugary drink free Pacific by 2030' (Sundborn et al. 2014).

perceived to be taking more than their fair share. For paternalists, this offers an opportunity.

At a practical level, the problem for 'public health' paternalists is that taxes on tobacco and alcohol are already extremely high in most western countries, far exceeding any realistic estimate of the external costs. Although it is widely believed that non-smokers shoulder the costs of smoking-related diseases, the empirical literature clearly shows the opposite to be true. As Le Grand and New (2015: 61) acknowledge, 'the taxes on tobacco and cigarettes are more than sufficient to cover all the additional medical care costs incurred by smokers.' In fact, it is far from certain that smoking and obesity impose any financial costs on others once savings to the taxpayer are taken into account. Few wish to admit it openly, but premature mortality after the age of 65, when individuals take more out of the system than they put in, saves the government large sums of money in pensions, welfare and social care. This is significant because it is the *net* external cost, not the gross external cost that should be used to calculate a Pigouvian tax.

The negative externalities associated with alcohol are more far-reaching than those associated with smoking and obesity. They include significant social problems such as crime, disorder and unemployment as well as costs to the NHS. The gross costs to public services in England amount to no more than £4 billion per annum, however, which is much less than the £10 billion raised through alcohol duty (Snowdon 2015a).

All of this poses a problem for 'public health' paternalists who want ever-higher sin taxes. Their solution is to ignore savings and draw up cost-of-vice estimates which include gross costs that are neither external nor financial. These estimates are then presented to the public as if they were direct costs to the taxpayer. The inclusion of lost productivity, lost income tax and the intangible costs of lost years of life inflate the total by many billions of pounds despite none of these 'costs' being eligible.

Since pay is directly linked to productivity, the costs of being unproductive fall on the worker through lower wages, missed promotions and dismissal. Insofar as absenteeism negatively affects industry, businesses usually have 'coping strategies' which mitigate most of the cost (Møller and Matic 2010: 31). In any case, a cost to business is not a cost to taxpayers. Some studies have compounded this error by including income forgone as a result of premature mortality, but insofar as a person can incur a cost after death, the cost is clearly internal. Consequently, the World Health Organization recommends that lost productivity from premature mortality be excluded from calculations of this sort (ibid.: 54).

The same principle applies to the intangible cost of a year of life. Monetary valuations of a life-year vary enormously and can only be arbitrary. Whatever estimate is used, it should be obvious that the benefits of being alive and, therefore, the costs of being dead, fall squarely on the individual.

Finally, it is wrong to include income tax that is 'lost' when a person dies as a cost to society. People who take early retirement or choose to work part-time are not portrayed as a burden on others, and for good reason: failing to confer benefits on others is not the same thing as harming them.

A case can be made for including emotional costs, but they are problematic for three reasons. Firstly, it is difficult to put a monetary value on them. Secondly, there are very few actions that have absolutely no effect on other people in some form, even if only on their happiness. As Berlin (1969: 124) said, 'no man's activity is so completely private as never to obstruct the lives of others in any way'. The mere knowledge that an activity is taking place can be enough to cause psychic damage to some people. As Mill noted in *On Liberty*, the very existence of alcohol offended the prohibitionists of the UK Alliance and violated their vaguely defined 'social rights'. Taken to its logical conclusion such extreme sensitivity could only result in making 'all mankind a vested interest in each other's moral, intellectual, and even physical perfection, to be defined by each claimant according to his own standard' (Mill 1987: 158).[3] Thirdly, emotional benefits to third parties must be counted alongside the costs. There are some *positive externalities* from drinking, smoking and overeating, such as those of the non-drinker who appreciates his local pub, but these are no easier to quantify than the costs. Most externality analysis therefore tends to be partial by construction and extraordinarily difficult to calculate.

We shall return to external costs and what to do about them in a later chapter. For now, it is enough to observe

---

3 The words 'even physical perfection', coming after moral and intellectual perfection, suggests that Mill saw health paternalism as a less urgent threat than other forms of illiberalism in the 1850s.

that the sin taxes of 'public health' paternalists differ fundamentally from the Pigouvian taxes of economists. Paternalists are not interested in finding the optimal level of consumption because they believe the optimal level to be zero. They are not interested in setting taxes at a socially harmonious rate for the same reason. As such, their cost-of-vice studies are political weapons rather than serious cost–benefit analyses. They offer a partial view of inflated costs, many of which are not external, while ignoring savings and benefits.

Collating the gross social cost of an activity, including emotional costs and costs to users, can be justified as an academic exercise, but the estimates of 'public health' paternalists are rarely presented to the public as such. Instead, they are presented, implicitly or explicitly, as the direct financial tax burden imposed on individuals as a result of deviant behaviour. Reading *On Liberty* reveals that there is nothing new about this tactic. Mill listed various tenuous externalities that were cited by paternalists as justification for intervening in self-regarding actions. He found them unconvincing and, aware of the paternalists' motives for citing them, concluded that if 'grown persons are to be punished for not taking proper care of themselves, I would rather it were for their own sake than under pretence of preventing them from impairing their capacity or rendering to society benefits which society does not pretend it has a right to exact' (Mill 1987: 149).

Lawrence O. Gostin (2013: 23), a firm believer in paternalistic 'public health' legislation, is candid enough to admit that externalities are largely used as cover for action that is really directed at the user:

American antipathy toward paternalism drives policy-makers to try to justify interventions under the harm principle – to argue, for example, that secondhand smoke, increased medical costs, and lost productivity amount to harm to others and so are not purely self-regarding. Third-party harms are not imaginary, but the real policy intent is simply to ease the grave burdens of diabetes, heart disease, cancer, and emphysema. Health officials genuinely believe it is unwise for individuals to smoke, overeat, live sedentary lives, or do myriad other things that cause them suffering and early death.

That negative externalities are used by paternalists as an excuse for interference can be seen in the way they demand taxes be set far higher than the Pigouvian rate and demand excessive regulatory responses to questionable externalities. For example, Sydney shut down much of its late-night economy in 2014, arguably a disproportionate response to a handful of high-profile violent incidents in the city. More recently, authorities in London have closed down parts of the nighttime economy in response to a small number of (self-inflicted) drug overdoses.

Several countries have banned smoking in every conceivable indoor place outside the home on the grounds that passive smoking harms third parties. Such bans cannot be justified on economic or liberal grounds since many of these places are privately owned and people can choose to go elsewhere. It is an open secret that the real aim of such legislation is to make it more difficult for people to smoke. 'Common sense suggests that bans on smoking in public places are intended to discourage tobacco use,' write Gostin and Gostin (2009: 216), 'but they are usually justified by the risks of side-stream smoke'. Many commentators have pointed out that efforts to ban smoking indoors long predated the emergence of any evidence about secondhand smoke (Bell et al. 2010; Bayer and Fairchild 2004: 487; Berridge 2007). Their true intent starts to become clear when campaigners call for bans to be extended to outdoor places and private apartments where no third party could realistically be affected. It becomes still more apparent when e-cigarette use is included in 'smoke-free' laws and becomes glaringly obvious when American campuses and baseball parks ban the use of smokeless tobacco.

Advertising

Choice in the market is more likely to be welfare-enhancing if it is voluntary and based on adequate information. If purchasing decisions are driven by the seller's deceit and/or the buyer's ignorance, a form of market failure results from an *information asymmetry*.

'Public health' paternalists sometimes seem to view the relationship between an industry and its consumers as being akin to that between a wolf and a lamb. They stand in a long tradition of anti-capitalist thought which views the market economy as exploitative and coercive, with advertising being the mechanism by which industry tricks individuals into acting against their own interest. The theory is, as Roger Scruton (2015: 47) puts it, that 'man, in his fallen condition, is subject to the tyranny of appetite, because his appetites are not truly his, but imposed on him, magicked into him, by others'.

It is occasionally claimed that advertising is an infringement of liberty. Parmet (2014) argues that tobacco marketing is not a self-regarding behaviour and Van der Eijk (2015: 3) accuses e-cigarette advertisements of being 'potentially autonomy-undermining' on the questionable assumption that they trigger the desire to smoke. But if advertising undermines autonomy, it does so no more than any other form of free speech. It is no more 'autonomy-undermining' than an invocation to stop drinking or lose weight, and since paternalists do not want to ban those messages we must conclude that it is the product being promoted, rather than the threat to personal autonomy, that they really object to. While it is true that marketing is not self-regarding – it is obviously designed to have an effect on other people – it does not undermine liberty and cannot, in itself, cause harm.[4]

Advertising can be persuasive and clever, but it has no mechanism to be coercive. The claim that advertising

---

4 In a roundabout way, this is acknowledged by Parmet (2014) when she mentions Morgan Spurlock's anti-McDonalds film *Supersize Me* and says: 'Even if we accept that Spurlock created the film in order to influence viewers' consumption of fast food ... the film would still not be paternalistic because it does not in any way limit the liberty of the subjects it seeks to aid.'

undermines free choice – and therefore creates a market failure – is questionable from the outset. Influence does not equal compulsion. As Childress et al. (2002: 176) note, 'it is not sufficient to show that social-cultural factors influence an individual's actions; it is necessary to show that those influences render that individual's actions substantially non-voluntary'.

Tellingly, paternalists seldom admit to being manipulated by advertising themselves; it is always other people – the 'less educated', 'vulnerable' or 'deprived' – who are susceptible. But if advertising is such an effective means of changing people's behaviours, why are health education campaigns not more effective? Unlike commercial campaigns for food and drink which promote specific brands, health campaigns explicitly promote behavioural change. If the behaviours they promote reflect the public's true preferences, as 'public health' paternalists claim, they should be knocking at an open door. Yet mass media campaigns to encourage healthier living produce only modest results (Jepson et al. 2010; Allara et al. 2015).

The consensus among economists is that advertising affects the distribution of sales between companies but does not affect overall demand. Consequently, as Julian Simon concluded after studying the subject for many years, advertising is 'not deserving of great attention' (Simon 1970: 285). With the exception of marketing for new product lines which alert consumers to the product's existence, advertising follows demand, it does not create it. The failure of advertising to increase aggregate demand in mature markets has been shown in real world studies of a diverse range of goods in many different countries (Yasin 1995). It would be strange if 'sin' products were any different, and since cigarette advertising does not increase consumption (Kenkel et al. 2015), it should be no surprise that bans on cigarette advertising do not reduce consumption (Lancaster and Lancaster 2003; Qi 2013). Nor should it be a surprise that alcohol consumption is not influenced by the ad spend of drinks companies (Wilcox et al. 2015). Companies spend money on advertising because it encourages brand loyalty, increases the value of brands and encourages consumers to try new brands. In short, they use it to fight for market share, not to enlarge the market.

This is the exact opposite of what 'public health' paternalists believe, perhaps because they view industries as monolithic entities rather than rival businesses. They mock those who say that advertising is not an important driver of behavioural change by asking rhetorical questions about why industry bothers to spend so much money on something that doesn't 'work'. Here is the pressure group Alcohol Action Ireland (2014), for example:

> Alcohol sponsorship of sports works in terms of increasing sales and, as a result, alcohol consumption. If it didn't the alcohol industry simply would not spend so much money on it.

One only has to think of heavily advertised products such as cat food, nappies and toothpaste to see what is wrong with this line of reasoning. In the 'public health' view, the only reason industries advertise is to increase sales and 'lure' new customers. But *industries* do not advertise.[5] Individual *businesses* advertise, and it makes financial sense for rival firms to fight for market share even if the market is flat or in decline. Imagine someone saying this:

> Cat food advertising works in terms of increasing sales and, as a result, cat food consumption. If it didn't the pet food industry simply would not spend so much money on it.

It is a laughable proposition and yet the same argument is taken seriously when it comes to alcohol and tobacco. Even politicians believe it, which is surprising when you consider how much of their own advertising at elections is based on getting consumers (voters) to switch from another brand (party).

Unless cat food advertisements encourage people to buy or breed cats, no amount of marketing for the product is going to make the market grow. Clever advertising might encourage people to buy more expensive cat food, but it cannot make them buy a greater quantity of it. And yet companies spend vast sums of money advertising essentials like pet food all the time. By the logic of Alcohol Action Ireland, they are wasting their money. So too are the alcohol companies, for that matter, since alcohol sales have been falling in Ireland for many years.

Simple assumptions about marketing stumble at the first hurdle. Yet the belief that advertising is the mechanism

---

5   Occasionally, industries work through trade associations to promote the whole product category, but these campaigns tend to be disappointing in terms of increasing sales (Schudson 1993: 25).

by which industry asserts its power remains strong, and there is a pocket of 'public health' academia dedicated to contradicting the economic evidence when it comes to alcohol, tobacco, food and soft drinks. Even with every statistical device at their disposal they find it difficult to show that adults fundamentally change their behaviour as a result of marketing; so their research focuses on claims about children and teenagers. It is said, for example, that teenagers who see a lot of alcohol advertising drink more alcohol (Snyder et al. 2006). It is also claimed that children who see e-cigarette advertising are more likely to become e-cigarette users (Singh et al. 2016) and may even be more likely to become tobacco smokers (Petrescu et al. 2016).

All these studies have one obvious and fatal flaw. They do not measure how much advertising teenagers actually *see*, only how much they *recall* – sometimes many years later. It should not be surprising that a drinker pays more attention to alcohol advertisements than a teetotaller and that a heavy drinker recalls more alcohol brands than a light drinker. People naturally have different interests, inclinations and upbringings. The kind of person who is interested in drinking, or grows up in a family of drinkers, will probably notice alcohol marketing more than someone from a different background.

That said, it is generally accepted that children are more susceptible to advertising, and pre-school children are particularly suggestible. At the age of five, with little understanding of marketing or the value of money, most children trust and like all advertising and more than half of them want every toy and game they see advertised. But it only takes a few years for them to develop the appropriate level of scepticism. By the age of 11, nearly all children understand advertising's persuasive intent and can distinguish between commercials and programmes. They no longer trust nor like all advertising and have 'acquired the general capability to recognise commercial persuasion' (Robertson and Rossiter 1974).

Up to a certain age, then, children are more myopic than adults and tend to be less cognisant of risks. The law recognises that children have diminished responsibility and we do not expect them to be fully informed and fully rational. However, since young children have little in the way of disposable income, their susceptibility to advertising is not a serious concern. Indeed, it has been plausibly argued that exposure to advertising in childhood is a 'necessary prerequisite for the development of cognitive defences against advertising's persuasive effect' (ibid.: 20). Since young children are not players in the market (beyond their influence on parents, sometimes referred to as 'pester power'), it is difficult to view their susceptibility to advertising as a market failure, but that has not stopped paternalists using the issue as a Trojan Horse to stamp out all marketing for 'unhealthy' products. As Bayer and Fairchild (2004: 486) note, campaigns to ban or restrict tobacco advertising were 'almost always focused on the claims of children' who were seen as 'vulnerable to the manipulations and seductions of advertising'.

Paternalists begin by arguing that advertisements for adult consumer products should not appeal to children. On the face of it, this is a reasonable demand. People who cannot legally buy a product should, perhaps, not be encouraged to do so. But as they define a child as anyone under the age of 18, this effectively requires a near-total ban. It is impossible to prove that an advertisement aimed at a 20- or 30-year-old will not appeal to a 17-year-old. In fact, it probably will, since teenagers want nothing more than to feel like adults. But when campaigners demand a ban on tobacco advertising in places that children will never go, such as nightclubs or cinemas showing 18-certificate films, it becomes obvious that young children's susceptibility to marketing is no more than an excuse for them to advance their real goal of suppressing commercial messages to every age group.

This comes at a cost. In addition to starving culture and media of valuable funding, advertising bans stifle information and impede free choice. This suits paternalists but it is the opposite of what would be intended if their concerns about voluntary choices were sincere. Whatever persuasive power advertising might have over those who cannot buy the product for legal or financial reasons is trivial compared to the genuinely coercive force used by paternalists to suppress it. By exaggerating the power of advertising, the paternalist diverts attention from the fact that it is he who is using coercion, he who is 'replacing one style of manipulation with another' (Scruton 2015: 47).

Children and addiction

An adult who is addicted to an activity can be said to have diminished freedom to choose. To some extent, his behaviour is involuntary. Combine the addict's inability to control himself with the child's inability to choose wisely and you have a potential market failure. Laux (2000: 422) argues that underage smoking 'influences adult behaviour and imposes an intrapersonal externality on adult welfare' as a result of dependency. In other words, the naive child enslaves his future self. Kessler et al. (1997) argue that 'adolescents are the gateway through which tobacco addiction enters the population.' In this view, the young smoker makes a decision at an age at which he cannot correctly assess the costs and benefits. In doing so, he curses his adult self with an addiction that undermines his decision-making forever. At no point, therefore, is his smoking ever a fully voluntary act. This narrative appears to be supported by surveys showing that most smokers start smoking before the age of 18 and that as many as 90 per cent of smokers want to quit.

Paternalistic action directed at both children and adults could be warranted under this scenario, but is a narrative that leaves so little room for human agency plausible? The claim that the vast majority of smokers become hooked in childhood and desperately want to quit is dubious. It is true that most smokers have their first cigarette before the age of 18 but, as Grill and Voigt (2015: 4) note, this does not necessarily mean they become addicted in childhood. According to the Health Survey for England (2016: table 7) 50 per cent of high-income smokers started smoking before they were 18, rising to 66 per cent among low-income smokers. This is a large proportion but not an overwhelming majority, particularly since the legal purchasing age was 16 when most of them started. And not all adult smokers are dependent; 40 per cent say they would not find it difficult to go a day without smoking (General Lifestyle Survey 2013). Evidently, there is a large number of smokers, including so-called 'social smokers', for whom the habit was not a 'paediatric disease', as some campaigners have labelled it (Kessler et al. 1997).

Since there are far more ex-smokers in the UK than there are smokers (55 per cent against 19 per cent in 2014 (ONS 2016a)), the habit is clearly not unshakeable. If smokers were hopelessly addicted to cigarettes, efforts to make them stop by raising prices would be totally ineffective. In fact, the price elasticity of cigarettes is similar to that of products which nobody claims are addictive, such as ice cream, flowers and toothpicks. And although it is sometimes claimed that 90 per cent of those who smoke wish to stop, this is an exaggeration. The Health Survey for England (2016: table 9) found that 33 per cent said they 'really want to stop smoking' in the near future, with a further 31 per cent expressing a weaker desire to quit. Thirty-eight per cent expressed no desire to stop smoking.

It is therefore true that the majority of smokers express a desire to quit, albeit with less fervour and in smaller numbers than is often believed. But stated preferences are unreliable, particularly when there is strong social pressure to conform. A smoker who says he wants to quit may be expressing a second-order preference (that is, he wishes he was the sort of person who didn't want to smoke) or he might be saying what he knows he *should* say in a society that disapproves of his habit.

Furthermore, when smokers are asked why they want to quit, the financial cost and social unacceptability of their habit feature prominently. But both of these problems have been largely created by anti-smoking campaigners with the express intention of deterring people from smoking (Hyland et al. 2004: 365). By using taxes, smoking bans and stigmatisation as artificial inducements to quit, 'public health' paternalists have changed the costs and benefits. As Phillips (2016b) remarks, an anti-smoking message that says 'Quit because it is so expensive and forces you to take breaks from hanging out with your friends' is no different from telling people not to take drugs because a conviction will affect their future job prospects. In the absence of co-ercive policies, it is reasonable to suppose that there would be fewer would-be quitters.

From the perspective of *rational choice theory*, the number of smokers who want to quit is zero; if they really wanted to quit, they would have done so. Some would say that their free will has been undermined by the addictive qualities of nicotine. But while addiction might change the costs and benefits, it does not render a cost–benefit analysis worthless, as Becker and Murphy (1988: 693) explain:

> The claims of some heavy drinkers and smokers that they want to but cannot end their addictions seem to us no different from the claims of single persons that they want to but are unable to marry or from the claims of disorganised persons that they want to become better organised. What these claims mean is that a person will make certain changes – for example, marry or stop smoking

– when he finds a way to raise long-term benefits sufficiently above the short-term costs of adjustment.

Becker and Murphy argue that addiction is not inherent-
ly irrational. People become 'addicted' when the benefits
outweigh the costs, and they quit when the costs outweigh
the benefits. In the case of harmful addictions, the likelihood of becoming addicted is greater among people who
put more emphasis on the present than on the future; this
explains why those who are experiencing stress, heartache
and bereavement are more likely to become addicted to tobacco, alcohol and drugs. The claim that addiction makes
people unhappy may be true in some cases, but Becker
and Murphy plausibly argue that 'people often become addicted precisely because they are unhappy' and 'would be
even more unhappy if they were prevented from consum-
ing the addictive goods' (Becker and Murphy 1988: 691).

We might take a more sympathetic view and acknowledge that many smokers genuinely struggle to give up
and that their autonomy is undermined to some extent
by nicotine's addictive properties. But taking a more sympathetic view does not mean giving more weight to vague
aspirations than to revealed preferences. If people really
wanted to give up smoking, we would expect them to express this desire strongly and make regular attempts to do
so. But an Office for National Statistics survey found that
only 22 per cent of smokers said they wanted 'very much'
to quit and only 26 per cent had made an attempt to quit
in the past year (ONS 2009). Making at least one attempt
to give up smoking in a year would seem the minimum

requirement for someone who really wishes to quit. And even if we give credence to stated preferences, we would expect smokers who 'very much' want to quit to say so. On either of these measures, the proportion of smokers who have a strong desire to quit appears to be closer to one in four than nine out of ten.

Addiction is a poorly defined concept. Some products appear to have addictive properties and yet most users never become addicted to them. Most drug users, drinkers and gamblers do not become junkies, alcoholics or compulsive gamblers. Stanton Peele, one of the world's leading experts on addiction, says that 'things aren't, in themselves, addictive' and argues that 'addiction is a constantly shifting cultural concept, not a biological entity' (Peele 2016). Leaving that debate to one side, let us assume that there is some proportion of tobacco and alcohol users who find it physically or emotionally difficult to reduce their consumption. Let us also assume that there is something inherent in tobacco and alcohol that makes compulsive behaviour more likely than with an average product. If so, it is an intractable problem, just as underage consumption is an intractable problem. In a society that allows adults to buy these products there will always be people under the age of 18 who get their hands on them and there will always be adults who become dependent on them. The question is how the government should respond.

Addiction and underage naivety are currently addressed by mandating warnings on packs and banning the sale of tobacco and alcohol to those under the age of 18. Both policies can be justified by conventional liberal and economic arguments, but 'public health' campaigners argue that much more should be done and invariably invoke children as their justification. Campaigners implore us to 'think of the children' every time they demand tax rises, advertising bans, graphic warnings, minimum pricing, plain packaging, licensing restrictions and retail display bans. Even blatantly paternalistic policies such as television censorship and outdoor smoking bans are proposed on the grounds that children should be 'protected' from the sight of people smoking. This tenuous justification for outdoor smoking bans is, as Leonard Glantz (2016) notes, 'an example of the extent to which public health advocates go to deny that their acts are paternalistic and to pretend that their actions are designed to protect others.'[6]

Paternalism is appropriate in the case of children, but that is what parents and guardians are for. Concerns about the welfare of children do not give paternalists carte blanche to pass coercive laws that have a negative impact on adult consumers. One can accept that youthful naivety and addiction restrict rational choice on a psychological level without supporting policies that restrict free choice in the most literal way. For example, a ban on the sale of tobacco to under-18s is uncontroversial but in some parts of the world this has been extended to under-21s. This is not on

---

6   Even some zealous anti-smoking campaigners have expressed their doubts about this policy. In 2000, the editor of the anti-smoking magazine *Tobacco Control* wrote: 'We need to ask whether efforts to prevent people from smoking outdoors risk besmirching tobacco control advocates as the embodiment of intolerant, paternalistic busy-bodies, who, not content at protecting their own health, want to force smokers not to smoke' (Chapman 2000: 95).

the basis that 20-year-olds are 'children' but because 'most adult smokers start smoking before age 21' (Campaign for Tobacco-Free Kids). Some 'public health' paternalists want to go further and ban anybody born after a certain year (usually 2000) from ever buying tobacco, a form of incremental prohibition that would eventually cover the entire adult population. Meanwhile, anti-tobacco policies which are said to be justified because they deter children from smoking and 'help smokers give up' (Parry 2015) are seamlessly transferred to food and soft drinks which are neither addictive nor age-restricted.

A society which permits any infringement on liberty in the hope of discouraging children and addicts is a society in which all adults are treated like children. 'Public health' measures ostensibly designed to deter some teenagers from making a decision which, due to their immaturity, might not be wholly rational, have a more profound effect on millions of adult consumers whose choices are constrained by law. It is not disputed that children and addicts will, at times, make decisions that fall short of the economist's vision of a perfect consumer. The problem is that paternalism takes everybody further away from that ideal.

Asymmetric information and health warnings

It is not paternalistic to require a seller to provide accurate information about his wares. Manufacturers and retailers usually know more about their products than do consumers, leading to information asymmetries. If they deliberately withhold important facts from consumers in order to make more sales it is arguably a form of fraud and is certainly a form of market failure. Free-market economists are therefore in favour of buyers being given the facts. Once equipped with adequate information, some people may decide not to buy, but that is not the economist's intention. The aim is only to give the consumer sufficient information upon which to make his decisions.

Information asymmetries due to consumer ignorance are a conventional market failure for which there is a simple solution: education. The state can have a hand in this by broadcasting information to the public, or mandating certain lessons in schools, or forcing manufacturers and retailers to impart certain facts to customers. Even John Stuart Mill approved of the use of coercion if a person was ignorant of the risks. In a much discussed analogy in *On Liberty*, Mill argues that it is right to stop a man crossing an unsafe bridge if there is no time to warn him of the danger, but that no one should intervene if he is aware of the risks. When there is 'not a certainty, but only a danger of mischief', he wrote, 'no one but the person himself can judge of the sufficiency of the motive which may prompt him to incur the risk' and so the person should 'be only warned of the danger; not forcibly prevented from exposing himself to it' (Mill 1987: 166)

Smoking, heavy drinking and overeating are activities which involve 'not a certainty, but only a danger of mischief' and there is always time to warn people. If their behaviour is the result of ignorance, we might expect a warning to have an effect. In the early days of cigarette pack labelling, health warnings helped to spread the word and convince

smokers that cigarettes 'may cause cancer' to current warnings that say 'cigarettes kill' and cause a variety of serious diseases and conditions. If we wished to have an informed smoking population, we would measure what smokers know about the risks of smoking. But success in labelling is not measured by what smokers know about the risks. Success is determined by the number of people who stop, or do not start, smoking. The goal is to control behaviour and have people do what we think is best for them.

In recent years, the slippery slope of regulation has led to cigarette-style warning labels appearing on other products. In San Francisco, sugary drinks are now labelled with the message: 'Drinking beverages with added sugar(s) contributes to obesity, diabetes, and tooth decay'. Thailand has recently introduced health warnings on alcoholic drinks. Some 'public health' campaigners in the UK would like alcohol containers to display the warning 'Alcohol causes cancer'.

It is not realistic to expect consumers to be *perfectly* informed about anything and there is not enough room on most consumer products for a label to provide every piece of potentially useful information. On a practical level, consumers who are given too many warnings might get 'warning blindness' and decide to ignore them all. This seems to be happening in California, where a vast number of products are labelled with the warning that they 'contain chemicals known to cause cancer and birth defects'. When health warnings are ubiquitous, consumers may find it difficult to distinguish between serious risks and minor hazards. 'Smoking causes lung cancer' and 'Alcohol causes breast cancer' are both evidence-based claims insofar as they reflect an increased risk of contracting the diseases, but the risk from drinking is small compared to the risk from smoking. Smoking causes around 70 per cent of lung cancer cases whereas drinking causes only around 6 per cent of breast cancer cases, and the evidence for the former is more robust than for the latter. Unless risks are put into context, there is a likelihood that consumers will make personal trade-offs based on an exaggerated perception of the hazards, which is to say they will consume less than would be optimal for them.

The risk of under-consumption does not concern paternalists, of course. The very idea that people could consume too little of a risky product would strike them as absurd. Consequently, their labels only ever tell consumers about bad news and are usually devoid of meaningful context. An informative warning for alcohol might explain that 11 million British adults drink at a 'risky' level, according to government statistics, and that there are 9,000 alcohol-related deaths a year, meaning that risky drinkers have a roughly 0.08 per cent chance of dying of an alcohol-related cause each year. If given this information, most consumers might conclude that a 'risky' level of drinking is not very risky at all. For that reason, such warnings are never issued. Instead, the public is told that alcohol has been 'linked to' more than 60 diseases and that there is 'no safe level of drinking'.

Similarly, cigarette packs could be used to tell smokers that they will live nearly as long as people who have never smoked if they quit before the age of 40, but as this would not deter – and could even encourage – young people to take up the habit, this factually correct information is shelved in favour of the simple message that 'Smoking Kills' (Jha and Peto 2013). Smokers and non-smokers alike tend to overestimate the risks of smoking. If they had a better grasp of the statistics, there would probably be more smokers (Viscusi and Hakes 2008) but, for obvious reasons, health campaigners have not attempted to correct that particular information deficit.

How much information should be mandated by the state and how much should be sought out by the consumer? For the products which concern us here, the basic facts are universally understood, namely that long-term smoking increases the risk of many serious diseases, too much food and too little exercise cause obesity, and drinking too much damages the liver. If people know this, they arguably know enough to make an informed decision even if they are fuzzy on the details. Further information is available in newspapers, online, from friends, in schools and in GP surgeries. It is not obvious that each and every health risk needs to be posted on the product itself, nor can it be assumed that people would reduce their consumption if they were fully versed in the facts.

If tobacco regulation is any guide, future labelling in the name of 'public health' will not lead to consumers being better informed. Graphic health warnings are less about education than they are about shock and disgust. Studies have shown that pictorial warnings are less effective in transmitting facts than written warnings because they literally repel the consumer (Leshner et al. 2010, 2011). Cass Sunstein (2014a: 139) supports graphic warnings as a way 'to persuade, not merely inform', but when the evidence was independently reviewed, it found that 'the impact of picture health warnings was negligible' among young people in the UK (Wardle et al. 2010: 71) and had 'no discernible impact on smoking prevalence' in Canada (Gospodinov and Irvine 2004). The obvious explanation for this is that 'individuals are very well informed about the consequences of smoking, and therefore benefit little from further messaging' (ibid.: 17). Once again, we have a legitimate market failure (or *potential* market failure) which paternalists have failed to solve – and may have exacerbated – because their intention is not to inform but to deter.

Summary: 'public health' as hard paternalism

We have seen that 'public health' paternalists use a series of arguments familiar to economists to justify government intervention. All of them imply some form of market failure due to consumer ignorance or irrationality. Some are based on flimsy assumptions, such as an unrealistic view of advertising. Others are more credible, such as information asymmetries and the irrationality of children, but 'public health' paternalists take these concerns much further than is necessary to improve the market. Taxes are used to deter consumption rather than to optimise consumption. Shock tactics are used in preference to information. Children are used as an excuse to restrict the free choice of adults.

It is difficult to avoid the conclusion that 'public health' paternalists are not interested in correcting market failures. They are doing something quite different. They are using taxes and regulations to change the costs and benefits of the activities they wish to discourage. Their policies generally involve regulating the product rather than regulating the individual, but the effect is much the same. The consumer is taxed, inconvenienced and stigmatised, thereby raising the cost of consumption. At the same time, the product is degraded, thereby reducing the benefits. The degradation can be subtle, as with packaging controls, or more obvious, as with mandatory product reformulation (such as sugar reduction in food and bans on flavours in cigarettes).

This is a far cry from education and persuasion. It is, to be blunt, cheating. It is disingenuous to claim that you are not interfering with free choice if you are changing the costs and benefits. By lowering the quality of the product and raising the price, the government is putting its thumb on the scale. If politicians use tax to double the price of chocolate bars and force manufacturers to cut their sugar content by half, sales of chocolate bars are likely to fall while sales of substitute products, such as apples, are likely to rise. But it would be untruthful to claim that consumers have suddenly decided to follow their 'true' preference for apples over chocolate.

With the rhetoric stripped away, 'public health' paternalism can be seen as a hard form of ends paternalism, which relies on assumptions about people's true preferences that are not supported by observed behaviour or even, in most cases, by stated preferences. Like Sarah

Conly, these paternalists assume that the optimal level of smoking, obesity and 'binge-drinking' is zero and, therefore, that the state must make every effort to drive rates down. There is an implicit, and sometimes explicit, belief that activities such as smoking and heavy drinking are irrational and provide no benefit to the individual.

These beliefs, combined with the assumption that health and longevity are all important, give 'public health' paternalists unshakeable confidence in the righteousness of their cause. Their conviction that both their means and ends are self-evidently correct manifests itself in the assumption that advertising is a powerful driver of behavioural change (why else would people act against their interests?), in the belief that those who do not share their values are in the pay of industry (why else would they deny obvious truths?) and that people are powerless in the face of 'social determinants'.

But despite the efforts of 'public health' campaigners to convince the public that personal responsibility is a myth and that lifestyles are dictated by environmental factors, many people remain sceptical (Buchanan 2008: 4). Since most people are not obese, do not smoke and do not drink excessively, they find it difficult to believe that other people are unable to resist temptation. The idea that individuals are powerless in the face of advertising and cannot resist affordable food and drink does not ring true for most people. The millions of people who have given up smoking or lost weight do not find it easy to believe that others are incapable of doing the same. 'Public health' paternalists, wedded to social determinism and looking at populations instead of individuals, cannot bring themselves to admit that they might have a point.

The claim that 'public health' paternalists are helping people to realise their true selves is at odds with billions of revealed preferences that can be observed daily. That so many 'public health' policies require punitive taxes and strict enforcement of an ever-growing pile of legislation is a strong indication that 'public health' paternalists are forcing individuals to act against their desires. These laws create negative externalities and many of them, such as tax hikes and smoking bans, have the effect of making individuals' choices decidedly *less* voluntary. Consumer sovereignty is restricted when advertising is outlawed and, as Mill (1987: 171) pointed out, '[e]very increase of cost is a prohibition to those whose means do not come up to the augmented price'.

Put simply, 'public health' paternalists deal with legitimate concerns about free choice by restricting choice further, and deal with minor market failures by creating major market failures. Ostensibly, these campaigners have a shared interest with liberal economists in ensuring that consumers are as informed, rational and free as possible, but as this is incompatible with their goals – such as creating a 'tobacco free world' – their solutions involve giving people less freedom.

8 THE CONSEQUENCES OF HARD PATERNALISM

To recap, traditional paternalism assumes that people do not always know what is best for them and therefore need the guiding hand of another. Nudge paternalism assumes that people *do* know what is best for them but fail to act accordingly because of psychological tics. 'Public health' paternalism assumes that people generally know what is best for them but are unable to act on their 'true' preferences because their environment makes it too difficult. The supposed environmental obstacles include such things as 'food deserts'[1] and a lack of cycle lanes but, above all, they include businesses making unhealthy activities cheap, convenient and attractive.

To reduce consumption of risky products, 'public health' paternalists therefore target 'the three As' – affordability, availability and advertising.[2] These 'environmental drivers' have long been the targets of temperance and anti-tobacco campaigners. More recently, they have become the focus

---

1 A 'food desert' is a place which does not have easy access to healthy food (e.g. fruit and vegetables). There is scant evidence of the existence of food deserts in Britain (Lyons and Snowdon 2015a: 24–25).

2 With tobacco advertising banned in many markets, tobacco control campaigners have changed 'advertising' to 'acceptability'.

of obesity campaigners, particularly with regard to sugar (Public Health England 2015: 40; Capewell 2014). In practice, the 'environmental drivers' of 'commercially driven epidemics' are basic levers of competition in a market economy (Adler and Stewart 2009; Britton 2015: 925). By portraying them as 'commercial determinants of health', paternalists foster the impression that industries are 'vectors of disease', with consumers as their powerless victims (Gilmore et al. 2011).[3]

Such rhetoric might be useful in a political campaign but it is intellectually hollow. The word 'determinant' implies a degree of inevitably about factors which are, at best, merely influences. In its most extreme manifestation, determinism implies that free will does not exist at all (one academic has mocked 'the illogical concept that individuals are in control of their behaviour in a manner that is something other than a reflection of their genetic makeup and their environmental history' and has called for the criminal justice system to be remade to reflect this (Cashmore 2010: 4503)). In reality, advertising and availability are a response to demand, not its cause. Tobacco and alcohol have been consumed on a grand scale for thousands of years, long before they were sold and advertised by transnational corporations, and people go to great lengths to acquire them when they are neither cheap, nor advertised, nor readily available (in prison, for example, or under Prohibition).

---

3   West and Marteau (2013) define commercial determinants of health as 'factors that influence health which stem from the profit motive'.

The claim that consumption is driven by affordability, availability and advertising is merely an inverted way of saying that people would not buy a product if (a) they did not have enough money, (b) it was not on sale, and (c) they did not know it existed. One might as well say that consumption is 'driven' by freedom since people do not buy products if they are prevented from doing so. Affordability and availability do not *drive* consumption. They *allow* it. The 'public health' response is to either forbid it or make it progressively more difficult.

If your only interest is reducing consumption, then policies aimed at undermining basic components of the market are not without merit. Advertising, as already discussed, is largely irrelevant to the overall pattern of consumption, but price clearly has an influence and 'public health' campaigners are quick to celebrate news that a tax has 'worked' whenever it has the (wholly predictable) effect of reducing consumption by a few percentage points, even if it has not improved health outcomes. Similarly, it is easy to imagine heavy restrictions on when and where products can be sold reducing consumption by making it at least inconvenient, if not physically impossible.

These policies rarely work as well as 'public health' paternalists predict because demand for tobacco, alcohol and food is generally inelastic. Taxes on food and soft drinks have had little effect on consumption, let alone on obesity, in every country that has experimented with them. Alcohol and tobacco taxes have been more effective but only when levied at a much higher rate. Restricting availability by artificially limiting the number of outlets does not reduce demand, it merely redirects demand to a smaller number of businesses. Conversely, increasing availability does not guarantee greater consumption. For example, alcohol consumption fell by a fifth in Britain between 2005 and 2015 despite 'public health' experts predicting that the liberalisation of alcohol licensing laws in 2005 would lead to a rise in consumption (Snowdon 2015b).

Nevertheless, it must be conceded that it is not difficult to put sand in the gears of the free market if the political will exists. The question is what are the consequences of doing so? Since supply is created by demand, efforts to curtail supply without reducing demand are bound to cause problems.

Higher costs for consumers

The most obvious cost of 'public health' paternalism is the tangible financial cost to consumers when prices rise as a result of sin taxes and, to a lesser extent, anti-competitive interventions such as advertising bans. Campaigners for higher taxes tend to portray the revenue raised by taxes as an additional benefit rather than a cost. It may feel that way for those who work for public sector organisations and quangos which profit from the tax revenue, but in practice it is a wealth transfer from individuals to the state. The money paid by those who consume the product effectively subsidises those who do not. In the case of minimum pricing, which raises prices without raising any additional tax revenue, the policy creates a simple *deadweight loss* with no offsetting benefit.

Of all the policies floated by 'public health' paternalists, sin taxes are the most popular with politicians and it is not difficult to see why. Most modern welfare states are in chronic debt largely as a result of ageing populations that have resulted from improvements in health. The average citizen pays less into the system than he takes out during his long retirement and pensioners are such a large and powerful voting bloc that reform is politically impossible.

The notion that National Insurance contributions build a personal nest egg is a fantasy. The welfare system is, in effect, a Ponzi scheme in which working people pay increasingly large sums of tax to support pensioners who have not covered their retirement costs. If demographic trends continue, the next generation will pay even more to support those who are currently working. This may be a price worth paying for longer lifespans but it is a cost nonetheless.

There is, therefore, a ravenous appetite across government for taxes that are politically acceptable and do not cause too much economic disruption. Sin taxes fit the bill and politicians can rely on a small army of campaigners in the 'public health' movement to lobby for them. Thanks to the pervasive, though mistaken, belief that smokers, drinkers and the obese are a drain on public resources, sin taxes are perceived to be equitable and so provide a rare opportunity to tax poorer groups in society, including pensioners, the disabled and the unemployed, without causing outrage. By demanding higher prices for unhealthy products, 'public health' pressure groups provide useful cover for politicians to raise taxes. One grateful Chancellor of the Exchequer, Nigel Lawson, remarked: 'Such is the success of the anti-smoking lobby that the tobacco duty is the one tax where an increase commands more friends than enemies in the House of Commons' (Lawson 1992: 65).

Sin taxes are a reliable source of revenue because the products targeted almost invariably have inelastic demand. Commonly cited own-price elasticities are –0.79 for soft drinks (Andreyeva et al. 2010), –0.46 for beer (Wagenaar et al. 2009) and –0.48 for cigarettes (Gallet and List 2003). Caution is recommended when dealing with such estimates as they vary enormously between studies but, on the face of it, these figures suggest that a 10 per cent increase in price reduces consumption of these products by 7.9 per cent, 4.6 per cent and 4.8 per cent respectively. Sin taxes therefore reduce demand somewhat – and so fulfil their ostensible justification – but not enough to lower total revenue.[4]

However, sin taxes are undeniably punitive for those who use the products. Alcohol duty (including the VAT on the duty) brought in £12.8 billion in 2015/16 (ONS 2016c) – the equivalent of nearly £500 per household. Tobacco duty (including the VAT on the duty) amounted to £11.4 billion, meaning that the UK's 9.6 million smokers were spending an average of £1,188 a year on this one tax (ONS 2016b). This is a significant amount of money to anybody, but when you consider that 23 per cent of British smokers have an annual income of less than £10,000 the regressive impact is laid bare.

---

4   The exception is tobacco duty, which hit the peak of the Laffer Curve in Britain in 2012. Since then, revenue from tobacco duty has fallen as the rate of duty has risen.

Sin taxes on food, alcohol and tobacco are so blatantly regressive that 'public health' paternalists have to resort to sophistry in order to justify them. One of the more peculiar arguments is that they are not regressive because they are optional. 'Nobody has to pay it,' said Sarah Wollaston MP of the sugar tax, 'so it's not regressive' (Glaze 2016). While it is true that sugary drinks are not essentials, the same could be said of almost any product that is subject to VAT and yet no one would seriously claim that VAT is not regressive. Regardless of whether people *have* to buy these drinks it is a simple fact that people *do* buy them and will continue to buy them with or without an additional sin tax. Furthermore, people on low incomes tend to buy more of them than do the rich. It is therefore inevitable that a sugar tax will be regressive (Muller et al. 2016).

Another claim is that sin taxes are actually progressive because the poor are most likely to suffer from lifestyle-related diseases. 'Poorer people would benefit more from a sugary-drinks tax,' says Simon Capewell of Action on Sugar, 'so it would be progressive in health terms' (Campbell 2016). This reasoning only works if the concept of regressivity is divorced from economics, where it has a clear definition (taking a larger share of income from the poor than from the rich) and applied to health. Even then, it remains dubious. It first assumes that taxes make people healthier and further assumes that people on low incomes are more inclined to lead healthier lifestyles when prices rise. The conspicuous failure of food and drink taxes to reduce obesity rates casts doubt on the first assumption and the high rates of smoking among the poor after decades of rising tobacco taxation cast doubt on the second (Hiscock et al. 2012).

If the concept of regressive taxation is to have any meaning it must include sin taxes on food, drink and tobacco. Whatever justifications 'public health' paternalists cling to, there is no doubt that these taxes relieve consumers of many billions of pounds each year, far exceeding the alleged costs of unhealthy lifestyles, and falling disproportionately on the poor.

Loss of consumer surplus

In 2014, the US Food and Drug Administration announced that it would be counting the pleasure of smoking as a benefit forgone by consumers who quit the habit as a result of tobacco control regulation. The agency had previously included *consumer surplus* in its cost–benefit analysis of graphic warnings on tobacco products and concluded that lost enjoyment offset 76–93 per cent of the predicted health benefits (National Institutes of Health 2013). Similarly, it estimated that mandatory calorie counts in restaurants would cost consumers between \$2.2 billion and \$5.27 billion over 20 years in pleasure forgone from eating energy-dense food (FDA 2014: 92).

'Public health' campaigners were outraged and appalled by the idea of including pleasure in impact assessments. The Campaign for Tobacco-Free Kids (2014) said that it was a 'deeply flawed approach' while Dick Durbin, a Democratic Senator, called it a 'ludicrous premise' (Begley and Clarke 2015). The most telling comment came from veteran anti-smoking activist Stanton Glantz who complained that acknowledging the benefits of tobacco use 'makes it a lot harder to justify regulations on cost–benefit grounds' (Begley 2014). To some people, introducing welfare economics into a health debate was self-evidently absurd. Dana Radcliffe (2014), an academic at Syracuse University, found comfort in the belief that 'ordinary citizens' could see that 'there is something seriously wrong with policy analysis that allows pleasures from unhealthy behaviour to be weighed against – and possibly outweigh – the health benefits of ceasing that behaviour.' And yet ordinary citizens make trade-offs between pleasure and risk all the time. Why shouldn't policy-makers do likewise?

Under pressure from 'public health' groups, the FDA watered down its plans (Begley and Clarke 2015) but the point remains. Putting a monetary figure on pleasure can never be an exact science, but the basic principle of counting lost consumer surplus should not be controversial. If consumers are rational, any increase in price is bound to reduce their consumer surplus. If they are biased or irrational in some way, the calculation should be adjusted to account for this, but the existence of bias does not justify ignoring consumer surplus altogether. Critics of the FDA from the 'public health' lobby wanted to quantify health while disregarding pleasure (Chaloupka et al. 2014: 4; Song et al. 2014). A standard economic model would do the exact opposite because, as Levy et al. (2016: 10) note, 'calculating health gains is redundant, because consumer surplus already reflects the consumer's valuation of any health gains resulting from the change in demand... there is no good reason why the welfare analysis of regulations that reduce smoking should begin by calculating health benefits.'

In fact, the FDA had more reason to include lost pleasure when looking at tobacco regulation than when it assessed calorie labelling. If calorie labelling makes a person change what they eat in a restaurant, it is because their previous choice was more fattening than they realised. Their revised choice better reflects their true preferences. Calorie labelling might create financial costs for the restaurant and it might create psychological costs for those who feel bad about ordering the least healthy option, but it does not create a cost for those who change their order as a result of being better informed. By contrast, if an individual is *coerced* into abandoning a pleasurable activity through bans, taxation or misleading information, he might enjoy a health benefit but will also incur a loss of utility (i.e. pleasure). This is a real cost and should be counted.

If the coercion fails and the individual continues to engage in the risky pursuit, he receives no health benefit and no welfare benefit. For example, a person who does not quit smoking after a smoking ban is introduced has to start smoking outdoors, often in unpleasant weather, enjoying himself less but incurring the same costs to his health. This is a net cost to the individual and such deadweight losses are the norm when 'public health' interventions are made. Since the paternalists direct their attention towards products that have inelastic demand, consumers are more likely to persist with their habit than to mend their ways. Dead-weight costs therefore affect very large numbers of people.

Some paternalistic policies are explicitly designed to reduce the buyer's consumer surplus. Banning menthol flavourings and reducing nicotine content in cigarettes amount to degradation of the product with the deliberate aim of making it less enjoyable. After deliberately ugly ('plain') cigarette packaging was introduced in Australia in 2012, 'public health' activists published a study which found that smokers perceived the quality of their cigarettes to have declined. Some smokers reported 'lower satisfaction' from smoking as a result (Wakefield et al. 2014). This was a psychosomatic response (the quality of cigarettes had not changed) but it was reported as evidence that plain packaging had been a success despite the fact that the study's participants had manifestly not stopped smoking.

Cass Sunstein supports graphic warnings on tobacco products but acknowledges that they impose a 'psychic cost' on smokers which could 'move an intervention along the continuum toward hard paternalism' (Sunstein 2014a: 57). Ed Glaeser, a critic of soft paternalism, argues that the stigmatisation of certain activities by the state amounts to 'an emotional tax on behaviour that yields no government revenues' (Glaeser 2006: 150). By making people feel that their behaviour is dangerous, disgusting or otherwise socially unacceptable, even educational efforts can lead to a loss of utility. Unlike a tax, which transfers wealth from the individual to the government, there are no offsetting benefits from the use of upsetting or stigmatising imagery. It is a deadweight loss (ibid.: 152–53).

Substitution effects

When prices are artificially raised by sin taxes, there is a halfway house between reducing consumption and spending more money. Consumers can switch to cheaper brands, shop in cheaper stores or turn to the black market. Instead of buying a premium brand of fizzy drink, whisky or cigarette, the consumer settles for a budget brand. Instead of shopping at a quality supermarket, the consumer turns to the discount store which sells the same brands but provides an inferior shopping experience. The same is true of the drinker who switches from the pub to the supermarket. If the consumer is close to the border, he might be able to shop in a cheaper country, but this takes more time and involves an *opportunity cost*.

There are endless opportunities for scofflaws[5] to outwit paternalists but all of them require a sacrifice of some kind. In each instance consumers can bypass the financial penalty of the tax but only at the expense of receiving an inferior experience. The substitute goods will be of lower quality than those previously purchased (or will be perceived as such by the consumer, which amounts to the same thing). Admittedly, there are some substitution effects that might improve an individual's welfare, such as switching to e-cigarettes and low-sugar drinks. If the individual freely chooses to switch after being informed that e-cigarettes are not as dangerous as smoking and artificial sweeteners

---

5   The word 'scofflaw' was the winning entry in a 1924 competition to devise a word for a person who continued to drink under Prohibition.

do not cause cancer, it could easily improve their welfare because people value health as well as pleasure. However, switching to these products under duress would probably lead to a loss of consumer surplus, assuming the individual to be reasonably well informed about the risks of each product.

Health has value and health concerns undoubtedly play a part in the trade-offs people make. If paternalists limited their activities to giving the public accurate information, all behavioural change would be positive. But since 'public health' paternalism is largely coercive, positive substitution effects are less common than the negative substitutions which might improve health but do not necessarily improve wellbeing. Instead, they reduce consumer surplus with no offsetting benefit. To put that in non-economic terms, they make life less enjoyable for no good reason.

The black market

At the extreme end of substitution effects sits the black market. The illicit trade depends on prohibition, over-regulation and excessive taxes for its very existence. Every increase in the price of legal products stimulates the demand for – and the supply of – illicit alternatives. If the goods are smuggled or stolen, there might be no loss of consumer surplus; on the contrary, the consumer could make a net gain since the illicit goods are cheaper but otherwise identical to the real thing. But often the products are counterfeited, homemade or otherwise inferior to legitimate brands. Moreover, the market is unpredictable. Quality changes over time and the consumer does not have the assurances that come with trusted brands manufactured and sold by law-abiding businesses.

The illegal narcotics industry is the most obvious example of a black market characterised by variable quality, price and availability. History is littered with examples of prohibition failing to prohibit, from alcohol in the US, to gambling in China, to marijuana nearly everywhere, but there is also a sliding scale of prohibition in which the problems associated with a total ban grow as the product becomes harder to acquire legally.

Countries with high taxes on tobacco and alcohol almost invariably have significant black markets. In New York, successive tax hikes on cigarettes in the name of 'public health' have resulted in smokers buying more than half their cigarettes in other states (Smith 2013). The UK, Ireland and France have the highest rates of tobacco duty in the EU and it is no coincidence that they also have the highest prevalence of non-duty paid cigarettes (KPMG 2015: 313). With their high rates of alcohol duty, the UK and Ireland also have non-trivial black and grey markets in alcohol, as do Scandinavian countries where alcohol duty is exceptionally high and home-distilling is relatively common. Price is not the only factor that drives illicit activity but there is a strong relationship between the (un)affordability of alcohol and the sale of untaxed drink (Snowdon 2012a).

If the UK's illicit tobacco and alcohol was sold at full price from law-abiding retailers the Treasury would have earned an extra £3.6 billion in 2014/15 (HMRC 2016: 33).

This is a loss to the state and a saving to consumers, but what are buyers getting for their money? The illicit product is often more hazardous to health than the legal alternative, with high levels of methanol and heavy metals in counterfeit alcohol and tobacco respectively. Furthermore, individuals incur the risk of arrest, fines and imprisonment when dealing in a market run by criminals. Having no legal recourse for settling disputes, black marketeers often turn to violence.

Despite the risk, inconvenience and uncertainty of dealing in the illicit trade, buyers must believe it is worth the effort, but they do not always have sufficient information upon which to base this judgement given the market failures that pervade the black market. We are not talking here about 'market failures' in the distorted, tenuous sense that 'public health' paternalists use the term but real market failures straight out of an economics textbook. Anti-competitive cartels and monopolies are common in the illicit trade. Rational and informed decisions are very difficult without the guarantees of basic product regulation and the assurances of quality brands. Black markets evolve to suit the producer, not the consumer, and dealers can make entirely false claims about their products without fear of legal redress. Moreover, there are significant negative externalities from criminal activity for which there can be no Pigouvian tax because the product exists outside of the tax system.

It is one of the ironies of 'public health' paternalism that it addresses questionable or minor market failures with regulation, which then leads to markets genuinely failing and products becoming completely unregulated.

Stigmatisation

If deviant groups are perceived to be a drain on the tax-payer, it is almost inevitable that public resentment will ensue. The resulting stigmatisation could be seen as an unfortunate side effect of 'public health' paternalism, but some paternalists actively welcome it as a necessary tool of behavioural change. In a blunt call for greater stigma-tisation of overweight people, Daniel Callahan (2013: 37) recollects that 'being shamed and beat upon socially was as persuasive for me to stop smoking as the threats to my health'. He argues that it is now

> necessary to find ways to bring strong social pressure to bear on individuals, going beyond anodyne education and low-key exhortation. It will be imperative, first, to persuade them that they ought to want a good diet and exercise for themselves and for their neighbour and, sec-ond, that excessive weight and outright obesity are not socially acceptable any longer.

Can state-sanctioned stigmatisation to encourage people to abandon risky, self-regarding behaviours ever be justified? Writing in *The Times*, David Aaronovitch (2016) claims that the 'indispensable driver' of the anti-smoking movement was 'to harass smokers almost wherever they went' but, in contrast to Callahan, he does not support a similar approach to fat people because it would produce 'more harm in the shape of disorders, breakdowns and bullying than it would gain in altering behaviour'. It is unclear how Aaronovitch can make this fine judgement. As Ploug et al. (2015) argue, we cannot measure the psychological costs of stigmatisation and it is therefore impossible to make the appropriate cost–benefit analysis. Erring on the side of caution, Ploug et al. conclude that 'using stigmatisation as a direct means to achieve public health outcomes is almost always ethically illegitimate'. Others have argued against the use of stigma more forcefully. Scott Burris, a professor of law, describes stigma as 'a barbaric form of social control that relies upon primitive and destructive emotions ... a liberal society simply ought not to be in the business of shaming its citizens' (Burris 2008).

Whatever the ethical arguments, stigmatisation in the name of lifestyle regulation is a reality. As Bayer and Stuber (2008: 48) note, the rise of the new 'public health' movement has seen 'a return to an older public health tradition, one that seeks to mobilise the power of stigmatisation to affect collective behaviour'. At first glance, this is surprising since the medical establishment has fought to remove stigma from drug users and AIDS sufferers, but this was because stigmatisation of these groups was seen to be counterproductive as it made them less willing to present themselves for medical treatment. Such concerns do not carry weight when it comes to smokers and the obese, who are more likely to be refused medical treatment than to hide themselves away.

In the field of tobacco control, stigmatisation has been rebadged as 'denormalisation' and is considered to be a thoroughly good thing. Referring to California, where smokers are second-class citizens in all but name, Gilpin et al. (2004) explain the denormalisation strategy in simple terms:

> In a society where smoking is not viewed as an acceptable activity, fewer people will smoke, and as fewer people smoke, smoking will become even more marginalised.

It is not just *smoking* that becomes marginalised under such a system but *smokers* themselves and it is they who ultimately become unacceptable. Many 'public health' paternalists are able to convince themselves that it is only the product that is being stigmatised but it is difficult to distinguish between a clampdown on an activity and a clampdown on a participant. Anti-smoking messages such as the NHS television advertisement which ended with the words 'If you smoke, you stink' are clearly directed at the person rather than the product.

In a 2008 article, Chapman and Freeman gleefully list the negative attributes that smokers are perceived to have in modern-day Australia, including the belief they are self-ish, thoughtless, malodorous, unattractive, undereducated and – inevitably – 'excessive users of public health services'. While acknowledging that a system of state-sanctioned demonisation creates psychic costs for those who fail to comply, the authors argue that the ends justify the means because, for the smoker, 'the obvious escape from this neg-ativity is to quit smoking'. There is also the added bonus that the dehumanisation of smokers 'foments a public climate that is highly receptive to tobacco control legislation' (Chapman and Freeman 2008: 30).

There is, however, a tension between the desire to stigmatise individuals and the strategy of blaming industry for people's lifestyle choices. If industry is to blame, then the consumer is a victim – and it is hardly fair to demonise victims. This is the line taken by most paternalists in the field of obesity who blame the food industry, government and the 'obesogenic environment' rather than the person who eats too much or exercises too little. Complaints about 'fat-shaming' seem to be at odds with the active 'denormalisation' of smokers, but this may reflect the fact that the anti-smoking campaign is at a more advanced stage than anti-obesity efforts.

It is fair to say that there are differing views in the 'public health' movement about whether stigmatisation is a legitimate political strategy, but regardless of whether this 'othering' of deviants is the intention of 'public health' paternalism, it is certainly the effect. Smokers who are refused surgery, denied the right to adopt children, turned down for a job or banned from smoking in their own home will not much care whether it is by accident or design that they have been disadvantaged.

Poorer health

The only justification for paternalistic 'public health' policies is the benefit to the health of individuals. It is therefore concerning that they not only often fail to achieve this but sometimes actively damage health. The unintended, though predictable, consequences of encouraging the sale of dangerous black market products have already been discussed. Sometimes, however, it is the *intended* consequence that creates the problem. Politicians, doctors, academics and pressure groups are not infallible and there are far-reaching implications when their opinions and prejudices are turned into law. Here are just a few examples of paternalistic policies being damaging and counterproductive:

- Many thousands of people were subjected to forced sterilisation in the US – and in California in particular – between 1907 and the 1970s for 'the protection of the public health' (Stern 2005: 1130). Eugenic theories and beliefs in 'racial hygiene' were often rooted in the doctrine of public health.
- For years, the British government taxed diesel at a lower rate than petrol to encourage motorists to switch to this supposedly cleaner fuel but it has since been shown that diesel fumes are more hazardous to human health.
- In 1992, the EU banned a smokeless tobacco product known in Scandinavia as 'snus' in the belief that it caused oral cancer. Subsequent research has shown that it does not cause any form of cancer but that it does work well as a substitute for smoking. Sweden became the only EU country to receive an exemption from the ban in 1995 and now has the lowest smoking rate in the developed world. Smoking rates are three or four times higher in other EU countries.
- In Australia and New Zealand, cyclists are forced to wear helmets on the assumption that it makes them

safer. Helmets certainly reduce the risk of serious head injury if the cyclist is in an accident, but it has been suggested that cyclists take more risks when wearing a helmet and motorists drive closer to those who are wearing them (Adams and Hillman 2001). This is difficult to prove either way, but there is no doubt that laws mandating cycle helmets reduce the number of cyclists on the road because not all bicycle owners are prepared to buy or wear one (Robinson 1996, 2006). This leaves those who remain more vulnerable to motor vehicles, since there is safety in numbers when it comes to cycling, and it takes an important physical activity away from those who are deterred (Jacobsen 2003; Wardlaw 2004).

- In 2011, Denmark put a sin tax on saturated fat. The tax was repealed after 15 months as a result of its negative unintended consequences but if it had succeeded in shifting consumption from fat to carbohydrates there are many who believe it would have exacerbated obesity and other health problems.
- E-cigarettes are banned in many countries, including Singapore, Australia, Finland and Hong Kong, on the assumption that they encourage smoking. As with snus (see above), the evidence suggests quite the opposite: they are used by smokers as a way of quitting.

Past mistakes do not mean we should disregard expert advice. As knowledge progresses, the scientific consensus can change. To take one of many examples, parents have long been told to avoid giving young children peanuts to prevent them from developing peanut allergies. Studies have since shown that children are considerably more likely to develop allergies to peanuts if they do not eat them at a young age. As a result, parents are now told to feed their children foods that contain peanuts before they are six months old (NIAID 2017). It would be unfortunate if children have developed peanut allergies as a result of the old advice, but the damage would have been multiplied if health professionals had found a way of coercing parents into following it.[6] It would have been bad for liberty, bad for health and a breach of the Hippocratic rule: 'First, do no harm'.

Given the risks of government failure and the fact that an individual who chooses to ignore health advice will generally only harm himself, it would be better to permit what Mill called 'different experiments of living' than to enforce expert opinion upon everyone which, if wrong, would magnify the consequences of error many times over.

There is also the question of how to best use limited resources. A pound spent campaigning for a sugar tax is a pound that cannot be spent on mosquito nets. 'Public health' paternalists use imaginative rhetoric to persuade us that Western lifestyle habits are as great a threat as hunger and infection, but comparing businesses to mosquitos and redefining obesity as malnutrition cannot mask the difference between a child dying from typhoid and an elderly man dying from heart disease.

---

6   With the rise of 'peanut-free' environments, such as classrooms and aeroplanes, it could be argued that parents have indeed been subject to a degree of coercion.

The World Health Organization has been particularly culpable in this regard. Formed in 1948, the WHO initially focused on such diseases as polio, smallpox and tuberculosis. Over time, as infectious diseases began to be wiped out in rich countries, the agency became increasingly preoccupied with non-communicable diseases and the lifestyle factors that supposedly drove them. The WHO had always received funding from governments in the developed world but it now became increasingly reliant on wealthy philanthropists from developed countries who were allowed to earmark their donations for specific projects. With the exception of HIV/AIDS, these projects tended to reflect the concerns rich Westerners had about diseases of old age and the lifestyle habits that were associated with them. For example, the billionaire Michael Bloomberg, who became synonymous with the 'nanny state' when he was mayor of New York City, gave the WHO $220 million for anti-smoking activities and later provided campaigners in Mexico $16.5 million to lobby for a tax on soft drinks.

After Margaret Chan became Director-General of the WHO in 2007, the agency adopted tub-thumping, anti-capitalist rhetoric more suited to a student union than an august United Nations agency. Chan named 'Big Food, Big Soda, and Big Alcohol' in her list of perceived enemies and blamed rising obesity rates on the 'failure of political will to take on big business' (Chan 2013). In recent years, the agency has extended its mission to push for a clamp-down on food advertising, restrictions on the portrayal of tobacco in films, taxes on soft drinks and bans on smoking outdoors.

Having no legislative power, the WHO is in danger of becoming a glorified lobby group as it seeks to persuade governments around the world to introduce paternalistic lifestyle regulation at the expense of tackling the infectious diseases which continue to plague developing countries. A symbolic manifestation of this came at the peak of the Ebola outbreak in October 2014. With the WHO under heavy criticism for its feeble response to the epidemic, a spokesman delivered a short speech on Margaret Chan's behalf. Apologising for Chan's inability to deliver the speech personally, he explained that she was 'fully occupied with coordinating the international response to what is unquestionably the most severe acute public health emergency in modern times' (Chan 2014). In fact, she was in Moscow attending a WHO conference on tobacco control, attacking e-cigarettes and congratulating Vladimir Putin on his anti-smoking programme (FCTC 2015).

It would take a moral cretin to miss the distinction between a health hazard which kills people at a young age through no fault of their own and one which shortens life by a few years as a result of lifestyle choices that are freely made. Until the day that infectious diseases are eradicated, diverting resources from the former to the latter is ethically dubious. Even in rich countries, where contagious diseases are relatively rare, it is doubtful whether the money spent on largely unsuccessful attempts to make people change their lifestyles would not be better spent on health and social care. For those who want medical help but are neglected because resources have been shifted towards lifestyle regulation, 'public health' is a cost.

External costs

Finally, there are the costs that do not only affect the targeted group but also fall on the general taxpayer. The costs of implementing and enforcing 'public health' legislation amount to a large and growing burden on taxpayers that could be avoided. There are also indirect costs if 'public health' measures successfully increase longevity. Thanks in part to lower smoking rates and healthier lifestyles, the retirement age will soon be increased to 68 and is expected to increase further as the century proceeds. This is a real externality to compete with the largely fallacious externality of unhealthy people draining the NHS.

Moreover, the whole 'public health' enterprise uses significant public funds to keep itself afloat. The budget of Public Health England alone amounts to £4 billion per annum (Public Health England 2016). Dozens of Public Health Directors are scattered around local authorities on six figure salaries (Taxpayers' Alliance 2016) and there are countless 'public health' activists and academics on the government's payroll working for quangos and universities.

In addition, there is a surprisingly large network of charities and pressure groups agitating for lifestyle regulation while being largely, and sometimes entirely, funded by the state (Snowdon 2012a, 2014). Similar networks emanate from the European Commission and World Health Organization. The 'public health' movement has become a state-subsidised industry. Although its employees claim that their work ultimately saves the government money by preventing disease, the economics of preventive health do not support this (Russell 2009; Bonneaux et al. 1998; Rappange et al. 2010).

9 TOWARDS BETTER REGULATION

Before we discuss how products should be regulated in a liberal society, let us recap on some of the key themes from previous chapters.

- In the secular liberal tradition, it is generally agreed that coercing people away from their preferred choices is unethical *if it is done solely for their own good*. Means paternalism can be justified under some circumstances but ends paternalism cannot.
- People have different tastes and preferences. It cannot be assumed that everybody has the same life goals (ends) and even when people have broadly similar aspirations, it cannot be assumed that they favour the same path towards them (means). Nor can it be assumed that one aspiration is more important than a competing aspiration.
- Revealed preferences are more reliable than stated preferences as a barometer of a person's desires unless there are compelling reasons to believe that a person's actions are substantially non-voluntary.
- The aim of policy should therefore be to make people's decisions about self-regarding behaviour as voluntary (i.e. free) as is practical.

There are also four important facts that tend be overlooked when paternalists discuss risk and pleasure.

Reducing a person's enjoyment is a cost

This should be obvious, but just as health has value so too does pleasure. Health can be factored into economic cost–benefit analyses by giving a year of life a monetary value. In health economics, life years are sometimes adjusted for quality of life but, consistent with the *health über alles* approach, 'quality' is defined only in terms of health. A disability is considered to diminish quality of life, but unhappiness and boredom do not.[1]

The firestorm that erupted when the FDA included lost pleasure in its analysis of food and tobacco regulation (see previous chapter) indicates how strange and foreign the idea of consumer surplus is in 'public health'. Nevertheless, it is fundamental. When economists talk about maximising utility, they are talking about the pursuit of happiness, fulfilment and satisfaction. Health, freedom and money are only means to that end. They are not an end in themselves.

Perfection is neither possible nor desirable

Almost any government intervention could be justified if market failure was defined so broadly as to encompass all

---

1   In 'quality-adjusted life years' (QALYs), health is assumed to be synonymous with utility (Prieto and Sacristán 2003).

scenarios in which consumers are not perfectly informed. Not only is it unrealistic to expect individuals to have perfect information, it is also undesirable. The effort required to become fully informed about every decision (the *search cost*) is usually too great. We do not need to know how every electrical device works. We only require it to function and be safe. For that we have regulation. For everything else, we have the advice of friends, family, shopkeepers, consumer magazines, the Internet, advertising and our own past experience. The advice does not need to be perfect, it merely needs to be sufficient for our purposes.

How do we know when consumers have enough information? A simple rule of thumb is that if providing more information would have no effect on consumers' behaviour – they know enough. Further information might be interesting, but if our aim is to ensure that people's consumption reflects their preferences, we need go no further.

Changing the costs and benefits is cheating

It is one thing to seek to persuade people that the costs of an activity outweigh its benefits but it is quite another to increase the costs and reduce the benefits in the hope of changing their preferences. An informed adult can make the decision to buy a product based on its characteristics and his own tastes. If the paternalist degrades the product's quality and hikes up its price, he is forcing the individual to weigh up an entirely different proposition. Anyone who abandons the product after it has been altered in such a way cannot be said to have changed his mind of his own free will; rather, he has had an option taken away from him by force.

A paternalist can educate, lecture, warn or even nag people about their lifestyle habits but he has no right to change the incentives. Any activity can be curtailed if costs and benefits are altered enough, but it would be coercive. Recall Thaler and Sunstein's rule that a nudge must not involve 'forbidding any options or significantly changing [the individual's] economic incentives' (Thaler and Sunstein 2008: 6).

Influence is not coercion

Advertising is not coercive. Low prices are not coercive. Packaging is not coercive. The mere presence of a product on a shelf is not coercive. None of the so-called 'commercial determinants' determine anything so long as there is choice.

Advertising is much misunderstood and its powers are greatly exaggerated by paternalists, but even if the wildest claims were true – that advertising makes people behave in ways that they otherwise would not – advertising would not be coercive in any meaningful sense. It is undoubtedly true that advertising leads people to purchase brands that they otherwise would not buy, but this, too, is not coercive. It is persuasive, and that is its intent, but the advertiser can only hope to persuade us to try a product once. It cannot make us continue to buy a product. For that, we need to like it.

By contrast, a ban on advertising is unambiguous legal coercion, a form of censorship that infringes the rights of businesses to tell people about their products and impedes the ability of consumers to acquire information. Earnest warnings about 'power', 'exploitation' and 'manipulation' by businesses in a competitive market are so much rhetorical chatter. Unless consumers are being deceived, their autonomy cannot be undermined by words and pictures, nor is their sovereignty eroded by deep discounting, two-for-one offers or colourful packaging.

If the aim of policy is to make people's choices as free as possible, artificially raising prices and banning truthful messages does not take us closer to that goal. Rather, it is a form of legal coercion that takes us further away.

Is there a better way? I think there is. With the principles of liberalism laid out in the preceding chapters in mind, I now offer suggestions for how controversial lifestyle products should be regulated in the UK. Most of the reforms I recommend require either a change in policy or simple repeal. I will focus on the five categories that preoccupy 'public health' paternalists – food, soft drinks, alcohol, tobacco and e-cigarettes.

Education and labelling

Goal: To allow consumers to make informed decisions

Health education is uncontroversial, particularly in schools. I have no advice for educationalists other than that information should be accurate and credible. The shock tactics that are sometimes employed to scare teenagers away from drugs have a tendency to backfire when the propaganda clashes with lived experience.

Out of school, there is a place for the government to run campaigns about everyday health issues, including drinking, smoking, diet and physical inactivity, if they are based on irrefutable evidence and address a genuine information asymmetry. It should go without saying that state-funded education programmes should not be designed to stigmatise individuals who do not conform to the 'public health' ideal. The government cannot make people like each other, but nor should it deliberately foster division and resentment.

Legislators should never forget that the aim of education is to inform. It is not, in itself, to deter purchase or to socially engineer. Governments ought to be as happy to use their resources to debunk popular myths, such as the idea that genetically modified food is unsafe or that e-cigarettes are as dangerous as smoking, as they are to hammer home risks.

Commandeering private property in the name of education raises more difficult questions. A high bar should be set for any government wanting to place its messages on a company's advertisements or products. There are so many public channels of communication for health education that it is rarely necessary to take over private spaces. To do so not only impinges on free speech, but amounts to forcing companies to say things that they may not believe, such as that there is 'no safe level of drinking'. To justify compulsion, the government must be able to show that its scientific evidence is beyond reproach and that the information cannot be imparted to the public by other means.

Politicians should be guided by two questions when considering whether to use the apparatus of the state to telegraph some new fact or other: 'Do the public already know this?' and 'Will people behave differently if they are told?' If they already know it, they are unlikely to act differently if told again, but even if the information is fresh it may still not change behaviour. If people do not act differently when told a new fact, it is reasonable to assume that they were already acting in accordance with their preferences.

So much information is passed around by civil society (e.g. friends, family, newspapers, television) as well as by those who work for the state (e.g. doctors, teachers, politicians) that nationwide media campaigns directed from Whitehall are rarely necessary. Informal networks do not always transmit information perfectly and yet they function well enough for the majority of people to be reasonably well informed about the essentials. The man on the Clapham omnibus does not need to understand germ theory to know that cleanliness is important, nor does he need to know what alcohol does to the liver to know that heavy drinking is bad for him.

Occasionally, a new health threat emerges and a mass media campaign is appropriate. The emergence of AIDS in the 1980s is one example. Swine flu and SARS are arguably two others, although the alarmist response to all three of these epidemics was probably excessive.[2] In the

---

2   Unlike swine flu and SARS, HIV/AIDS became a major public health problem, but the threat of a major AIDS pandemic among heterosexuals was never as likely as government health warnings implied (Fitzpatrick 2008).

field of lifestyle regulation, only the smoking–cancer link has required a similar educational effort since smoking was so widespread in the mid-twentieth century and so many people were sceptical about the 'tobacco scare' (as it was sometimes known). In that instance, special warnings on the product could be justified since they provided an official stamp of authority to a health claim that was still contested, not least by the tobacco industry. The warnings were all the more powerful for being unusual. The very fact that no other consumer product was emblazoned with such a warning made the public take it seriously.

An argument could be made for further labelling on other products if there is good evidence that (a) large parts of the public are misinformed about certain risks, (b) those risks are meaningful and well-proven, (c) the warnings would make a difference to patterns of behaviour, and (d) it is not possible to effectively transmit the information by other means. In most cases, however, the case for warning labels fails to meet at least one of these criteria.

Food

People have a right to know what they are putting in their body and so food labelling is relatively uncontroversial. Ingredients have been listed on food products for many years and most processed food in Britain uses a 'traffic light' system of red, amber and green to signal nutritional quality as part of a voluntary agreement between industry and government. Food labelling is an EU competence so member states cannot legislate alone, but outside of the EU the government could bring in mandatory traffic light labels. Though simplistic and somewhat arbitrary, they arguably help consumers to make better buying decisions at a glance *when comparing similar items*. If the government was to go down this path it would need to ensure that the costs are low and smaller companies are exempt. It should also use a consistent system showing the number of calories per product rather than the number of calories per 100 grams or per serving as manufacturers have a tendency to understate the size of a typical serving.

Calorie labelling on packaged food and drink products is difficult to argue with. It is harder to defend the idea of displaying sugar content in teaspoons, as some have suggested. This would create a negative signalling effect by implying that calories from sugar are somehow more fattening than calories from other sources. This might be in keeping with the current hysteria about sugar but any labelling that suggests that obesity is caused by a single nutrient is likely to mislead the public.

A more scientifically robust idea is compulsory calorie labelling in restaurant chains. When this was introduced in New York it led to more awareness of the calorie content of food and soft drinks but had no effect on the number of calories consumed (Elbel et al. 2011; Cantor et. al. 2015). Earlier field experiments also found no effect on behaviour (Ellison et al. 2014). The case for mandatory calorie counts therefore looks weak on both economic and paternalistic grounds although it could be argued that consumers still have a right to know. Displaying calorie content is unlikely to incur psychic costs on consumers since the information does not hector or stigmatise. The business costs will be low for chain restaurants and processed food manufacturers, but higher for cafés, pubs and small shops which sell less homogeneous dishes. If there were to be any legislation, these businesses should be exempt.

There are currently murmurings about placing health warnings on sugary drinks. In San Francisco, fizzy drinks come with a label cautioning that their consumption can lead to obesity and diabetes. This is an absurdity. Obesity is a risk factor for diabetes and too many calories from sugary drinks can cause obesity, but too many calories from any source can cause obesity. There is nothing special about the 139 calories in a can of *Coca-Cola* that makes people particularly susceptible to either obesity or diabetes. Unless the British government is prepared to label every food and drink product with the same warning, it should not follow California's lead.

In summary, mandatory food labelling can be justified but only if it provides people with neutral information about ingredients and calories without focusing on specific nutrients. Food products that have been deemed safe under basic food regulation cannot be considered dangerous and so food labelling should never resemble a 'warning'.

Alcohol

Just as consumers have a right to know what they are eating, they also have a right to know what they are drinking.

Calorie labelling should therefore be introduced on alcoholic drinks unless research finds significant unintended consequences.[3]

Further labelling should be resisted, however. The British public, we are told, are woefully ignorant about the link between alcohol and cancer, and labelling drinks with a cigarette-style cancer warning would be an effective way to spread the word. Perhaps it would, but the risks are so small in practice that such a system would either discredit scientific advice in the eyes of the public or alarm consumers to such an extent that they would make worse choices than if they remained ignorant. A truthful alcohol label would explain that associations have been found between alcohol consumption and several cancers, most of which are rare. It would explain risks in absolute, rather than relative, terms (e.g. 'Heavy drinking increases your lifetime risk of developing disease X from Y per cent to Z per cent'). Finally, it would explain that moderate consumption of alcohol reduces the risk of heart disease, stroke and diabetes, and that premature death is less common among moderate drinkers than teetotallers, although heavy drinkers have a higher mortality rate than either.

Aside from the fact that this is too wordy to fit onto a bottle of wine, a label that explained the science adequately would make consumers better informed whereas a warning saying 'alcohol causes cancer' would lie by omission. A truthful label would probably have no effect on alcohol

---

3   There are concerns that calorie labelling on alcohol could lead weight-conscious consumers to skip meals or switch to hard liquor.

consumption other than possibly increasing it. It is questionable whether it is worth putting it on the bottle at all, particularly since the information is available from other sources for those who are interested. And yet it is only the verbose yet truthful label, not the crude cancer warning favoured by paternalists, that can be ethically justified if the aim is to inform rather than alarm.

Cigarettes

Graphic warnings cannot be justified on any product. They are not educational in any real sense and have been declared unconstitutional in the US on the grounds that their objective is to create an 'emotional response' rather than disseminate 'purely factual and uncontroversial information' (Leon 2011: 14). Plain packaging has all the drawbacks of graphic warnings plus the unjustified removal of registered trademarks and should also be rejected. In the case of smoking, the health risks are so well known that there is no information asymmetry to be addressed. Even if people were ignorant of the risks, it is not obvious that replacing brand logos with photos of gangrenous feet is a more effective way of educating them than using written information.

Though largely obsolete in the twenty-first century, written warnings should remain on tobacco products because removing them might send a signal to some consumers that the scientific consensus on the health risks of smoking had weakened, but the 'psychic costs' and lost consumer surplus that result from the use of graphic images amount to economic costs for which there is no offsetting benefit. Legislation that enforces graphic warnings and plain packaging in the UK should therefore be repealed and similar legislation for other products should be rejected.

E-cigarettes and smokeless tobacco

E-cigarettes are an interesting case because they have been swamped by misinformation since they became popular in the early 2010s. Under EU legislation, bottles of e-cigarette fluid are sold with a warning about the addictive properties of nicotine. They must also be sold with a leaflet warning about the supposed dangers of vaping. This information is not necessarily untrue but neither is it helpful. Product labelling is a last resort for correcting information asymmetries. In the case of vaping, the popular misconception is that e-cigarettes are more dangerous than they are (ASH 2015). Existing warnings can only serve to deter people from vaping whereas if consumers were perfectly informed there would be more vaping (and less smoking as a result) (Phillips 2016c). A useful, evidence-based warning would explain that nicotine is addictive but that the risks of vaping are 'unlikely to exceed 5% of those associated with smoked tobacco products, and may well be substantially lower than this figure' (Royal College of Physicians 2016: 84).

Smokeless tobacco products are little used in Britain but exiting the EU would allow us to start selling snus (see previous chapter). If so, we should not make the same mistake as the US in sending a negative signal by concealing important information. Smoking causes hundreds of thousands of deaths each year in the US whereas smokeless tobacco causes a few dozen cases of oral cancer. Despite the dramatic difference in risk profiles between the two products, the Surgeon General insists on labelling smokeless tobacco with a warning that reads: 'This product is not a safe alternative to cigarettes.'[4] This is technically true, but lies by omission. A more accurate warning would explain that smokeless tobacco is approximately 99 per cent sa fer than cigarettes. If consumers were better informed in this way, it would lead to more smokers switching to smokeless products, thereby benefiting their health.

The intention behind the misleading warning labels is to dissuade people who do not currently use any tobacco product from experimenting with smokeless tobacco. The Surgeon General feared that people who are deterred from smoking by the health risks might be tempted to enjoy the benefits of nicotine if the risks were much reduced. Though plausible, this is surely a decision for individuals. In this instance, US authorities are deliberately withholding information because they fear that consumers will make the 'wrong' choice if the full facts are made available to them. They are acting paternalistically on the basis of two implicit beliefs, both of which fly in the face of lived experience – that the use of tobacco confers no private benefits and that no level of risk is acceptable.

---

4   One Surgeon General went further, publicly stating in 2003 that 'Smokeless tobacco is not a *safer* substitute for cigarette smoking' (emphasis added) (Carmona 2003).

The 'public health' justification for misleading consumers in this way is questionable on its own terms. Like e-cigarettes, smokeless tobacco is a substitute for a much more dangerous product: the combustible cigarette. It would require 100 non-smokers to start using smokeless tobacco for every smoker that switches to it for the net health impact to be negative. But even making this calculation is to accept the collectivist logic of 'public health'. From a liberal or economic perspective, what matters is that individuals are sufficiently informed to balance risk against benefits. A non-smoker might forgo the pleasures of smoking to avoid the health risks, but might rationally use other forms of nicotine if the risks were reduced.

The lesson from labels on smokeless tobacco and e-cigarettes is that information that is given special prominence on packaging can cause a negative signalling effect which misleads consumers even when the information is accurate. Since warning labels remain relatively rare, they are assumed to be required only when risks are unusually large, as with cigarettes. Campaigners against genetically modified organisms are keen to place labels on products which contain them. On the face of it, this is neutral information – the labels will merely say that the product contains GMOs – but in practice the label acts as a de facto warning: why would the government force companies to display this information if there was nothing to worry about (Lusk and Rozan 2008; Sunstein 2017)?

Assuming that the scientific consensus on GM foods is correct, such labels serve no purpose. If people were fully informed (i.e. if they understood that the risks from GM foods are 'essentially zero' (Sunstein 2016)), they would buy more of them. The labels are likely to make people buy fewer of them, even though the information on the label is not inaccurate. This negative signalling effect will move individuals further away from the ideal of the fully informed, fully rational consumer and it illustrates the risks of over-labelling. It is a measure that should only be used when the hazard is extreme and ignorance is widespread.

Taxation

Goal: To prevent third parties paying for other people's behaviour

Sin taxes can be justified if there are legitimate external costs borne by the state. A pure insurance-based health and welfare system would put an end to claims about unhealthy lifestyles being a burden on the taxpayer but so long as these services are paid for by the general taxpayer, sin taxes should cover the *net costs* associated with smoking and drinking: that is, the health and welfare costs minus the health and welfare savings.

In practice, these taxes would be much lower than at present. As discussed above, the net costs of smoking are negligible, if not negative, and so it is difficult to make an economic case for sin taxes on tobacco other than to fund stop-smoking services and anti-smoking advertising. The costs of alcohol consumption to public services do not exceed £4.6 billion per annum (Snowdon 2017). An equitable rate of tax on alcohol would therefore be less than half the current rate, bringing it broadly in line with the European average.

Alcohol taxation in Britain has evolved along protectionist lines with wine being penalised while cider is treated more leniently (though still heavily taxed by international standards). This is plainly an attempt to help British businesses at the expense of foreign producers. A Pigouvian tax would not discriminate. Alcohol duty should be a tax on ethanol, nothing more. It should tax units of alcohol, not the volume of different fluids. British drinkers currently consume around 50 billion units of alcohol per annum. To recover £4.6 billion in costs, there should be a flat rate of tax of 9p per unit on all alcoholic drinks. There could, however, be an argument for taxing some units of alcohol more heavily if it could be shown that one type of drink is associated with greater costs than another. EU law currently prohibits taxing alcohol by the unit, but it could be implemented post-Brexit.

Obesity is more difficult since it has multiple causes. No single product can be held responsible and physical inactivity cannot be taxed. Fortunately, the question is largely academic since the net costs of obesity are much lower than is often claimed (Tovey 2017).

Pricing

Goal: To provide the lowest prices possible

John Stuart Mill approved of taxes on alcohol and tobacco as a means of collecting necessary revenues for government. Indeed, he saw alcohol as a luxury that could be taxed to the peak of the Laffer Curve if the government needed the money (Mill 1987: 170–71). But he was against using taxes as a means of discouraging consumption and, in the same spirit, we can support the use of alcohol duty to compensate for negative externalities while opposing the use of pricing for paternalistic reasons. I am discussing pricing separately from taxation because not all paternalistic price policies involve taxes and to reaffirm that low prices are an unambiguously good thing. In an ideal world everything would be free. Sadly, we do not live in an ideal world and so the best we can hope for is for things to be cheap. If, as Mill argued, inflated prices are different to full prohibition only by a matter of degree, low prices are liberty-enhancing.

Setting a minimum price on a product, as has been proposed with alcohol, should therefore be rejected, not just because it is unnecessary but because it is regressive and imposes a deadweight cost on consumers with no offsetting tax revenue.

Controls on sale

Goal: To prevent transactions which are substantially non-voluntary

Many paternalistic policies are introduced on the pretext that they will reduce consumption by children. This is a powerful argument since nearly everyone agrees that adult activities should be confined to adults. However, the side effect (if not the intended effect) of much of this regulation is to negatively impact adult consumers. If a product is intended for adult consumption only, it should be illegal to sell to children and proxy purchasing (by adults for children) should also be forbidden.

Alcohol licensing laws in Britain have been much improved by the Licensing Act of 2003 and there are few restrictions on where food can be sold other than some quixotic restrictions on fast food outlets by local authorities. These serve only to limit competition, restrict choice and, in some instances, raise prices. Ostensibly introduced to prevent childhood obesity, they are ineffective token gestures which should be swept away.

Leaving the EU provides an opportunity to repeal various laws on e-cigarettes and tobacco which are not only illiberal but are counter-productive even from the perspective of a health paternalist. For example, behavioural economists regard cigarettes sold in packs of ten as a useful nudge to help smokers reduce their consumption and quit (Marti and Sindelar 2015). Cass Sunstein (2014b: 193) even suggests that it should be compulsory for retailers to offer cigarettes in small packs. Instead, the EU's Tobacco Products Directive bans them. It also bans the higher strength e-cigarette fluid that many smokers need to make the permanent switch from smoking. It bans most e-cigarette advertising and creates an expensive bureaucracy for the e-cigarette industry that has resulted in the range and quality of products diminishing significantly since the directive was implemented in May 2016. Its policies on tobacco, such as a ban on menthol cigarettes, serve no obvious purpose. The whole directive should be repealed along with homegrown anti-smoking policies aimed at disrupting the market, such as the retail display ban.

Advertising

Goal: To prevent consumers being deceived

In contrast to the countless words written about advertising by 'public health' paternalists, there is little to say about it from a liberal perspective other than that it should be truthful. Since its purpose is to persuade, we should not expect the unvarnished truth, but the Advertising Standards Agency's requirement that advertisements be 'legal, decent, honest and truthful' strikes the right chord. If a product can be legally sold, it should be legal to tell people about it, although the time and place in which it can be advertised could be regulated depending on the content.

The ban on advertising food that is high in fat, salt or sugar during children's programmes should be repealed. The ban was a major contributor to the closure of Children's ITV in 2006, thereby limiting viewing options for children after school (Holmwood 2006). The products in question are generally recognised as safe and the advertising is effectively aimed at parents watching television with their children rather than at the children themselves (the large number of advertisements for detergent and bleach shown during children's programmes is a testament to this). Children do not have significant purchasing power but they are rightly allowed to buy these products and so there is no good reason for trying to prevent them being seen on television.

Current rules on alcohol advertising are among the toughest in the world and there is a stronger case for them to be relaxed than tightened. Regulations prevent advertisers from suggesting things that are arguably true. They are not allowed to associate alcohol with 'seduction, sex or social success', for example, nor are they permitted to link alcohol with 'irresponsible' behaviour.

A total ban on tobacco advertising cannot be justified in a free society. The effect of banning advertising has been to keep out new entrants, prevent competition and raise prices. It is absurd that tobacco companies have almost no way of communicating with their customers, thereby making it virtually impossible to put new tobacco products on the market, even when those products are less hazardous than cigarettes. The tobacco industry has saved a fortune from the advertising ban, it is the consumer who has been disadvantaged. Television commercials for cigarettes were taken off the air in the 1960s as part of a voluntary agreement with industry and are unlikely to return, but advertisements should at least be permitted in adult-oriented print media, as in the US.

There could be counter-productive signalling effects from reintroducing tobacco advertising after such a long time (i.e. it might be assumed that smoking is less hazardous than previously believed) but this could be dealt with by strong health warnings on advertisements as well as counter-advertising paid for by tobacco duty.

Teach economics

One final point should be made before we end this mono-graph. Neo-paternalists cite evidence from behavioural economics to justify government intervention. Nudge the-orists and coercive paternalists alike tell us that cognitive biases in the human brain show that we are not as rational as John Stuart Mill assumed and, by implication, that we are not capable of making our own decisions. I have argued in this book that the insights from behavioural economics are not sufficient to undermine the case for individual lib-erty. Allowing flawed human beings to make their own choices based on their own preferences might not be per-fect, but nobody has come up with a better system.

This is not to dismiss the evidence from behavioural economics. Nobody claims that human beings are per-fectly rational. But there is a simple answer to those who herald the latest findings from behavioural economics as proof of humanity's incorrigible irrationality. If you believe that people would make better decisions if they were more rational, teach them economics. It is no coincidence that economists are more rational than the average person. It is an acquired skill. Most of the fallacies and biases that trip people up when making decisions are childishly sim-ple once explained. Only when you are aware of the pitfalls can you make an effort to avoid them.

I hesitate to join the queue of single-issue campaigners demanding additions to the curriculum, but it is strange that economics is so neglected in schools when the lessons are so handy in everyday life. Concepts such as the *sunk cost fallacy, hyperbolic discounting, opportunity cost* and *anchoring* can be explained in minutes and are useful for a lifetime. A wider dispersion of the lessons of behavioural economics, and of microeconomics generally, would improve many people's decision-making and, we might dare to dream, even lead to better policy-making.

GLOSSARY

Anchoring: A cognitive bias in which a person is swayed by the first piece of information they encounter and use it as a reference point. For example, inferring from a price label that says 'Was £30 – Now £20' that £20 is a good price.

Consumer surplus: The difference between the price a person is prepared to pay for a good or service and the price they actually pay. It is the benefit, or welfare gain, enjoyed by the buyer.

Deadweight loss: A loss of economic efficiency caused when equilibrium is not achieved, i.e. when the quantity supplied by the market does not match the quantity sought by consumers. Causes can include taxes, subsidies and price controls.

Ends paternalism: Leading people towards goals that a paternalist has set for them.

Heuristics: Mental shortcuts designed for quick and satisfactory, but not necessarily ideal, decision-making (see *satisficing* below).

Hyperbolic discounting: Valuing rewards in an inconsistent way when the costs and benefits are in the future. For example, a person may rationally choose to take £100 today rather than £150 next year, but given the choice between £100 in five years and £150 in six years, he may choose the latter. Since both choices require a twelve-month wait, this is inconsistent.

Information asymmetry: One party in a transaction knowing more about the good or service than the other party. Also known as 'information failure'.

Means paternalism: Helping people to reach goals that the individuals have set for themselves.

Negative externality: A cost of an economic activity that is borne by a third party. Also known as an 'external cost' or 'negative spillover effect'.

Opportunity cost: The value of something that is given up when a different course of action is taken, e.g. forgoing a day's salary to have an extra day's holiday.

Positive externality: A benefit of an economic activity to a third party.

Rational choice theory: An economic theory in which people are assumed to always make logical, welfare-maximising decisions.

Satisficing: A *heuristic* designed to find a satisfactory solution when the costs of finding a perfect solution are too great. Derived from a combination of 'satisfy' and 'sufficing'.

Search cost: The time and effort spent gathering the information needed to make a decision. Search costs can be minimised by *satisficing*.

Sunk cost fallacy: The mistaken belief that one should continue to spend resources on an inefficient project because one has already invested resources in it. The opposite of 'cutting your losses'.

REFERENCES

Aaronovitch, D. (2016) We need heavy weapons to win the obesity war. *The Times*, 28 July, p. 21.

Adams, J. and Hillman, M. (2001) The risk compensation theory and bicycle helmets. *Injury Prevention* 7: 89–91.

Adler, N. and Stewart, J. (2009) Reducing obesity: motivating action while not blaming the victim. *Milbank Quarterly* 87(1): 49–70.

Alcohol Action Ireland (2014) Banning alcohol sponsorship of sport is not just supported by the evidence, it is the right thing to do. http://alcoholireland.ie/home_news/banning-alcohol-sponsorship-of-sport-it-is-not-just-supported-by-the-evidence-it-is-the-right-thing-to-do/ (June).

Allara, E., Ferri, M., Bo, A., Gasparrini, A. and Faggiano, F. (2015) Are mass media campaigns effective in preventing drug use? A Cochrane systematic review and meta-analysis. *BMJ Open* 5(9).

Allmark, P. (2006) Choosing health and the inner citadel. *Journal of Medical Ethics* 32(1): 3–6.

Andreyeva, T., Long, M. and Brownell, K. (2010) The impact of food prices on consumption: a systematic review of the price elasticity of demand for food. *American Journal of Public Health* 100(2): 216–22.

Arno, A. and Thomas, S. (2016) The efficacy of nudge theory strategies in influencing adult dietary behaviour: a systematic review and meta-analysis. *BMC Public Health* 16(676).

ASH (2015) Electronic cigarette use among smokers slows as perceptions of harm increase. http://www.ash.org.uk/media-room/press-releases/:electronic-cigarette-use-among-smokers-slows-as-perceptions-of-harm-increase (22 May).

Bagnardi, V. et al. (2013) Light alcohol drinking and cancer: a meta-analysis. *Annals of Oncology* 24(2): 301–8.

Bayer, R. and Fairchild, A. (2004) The genesis of public health ethics. *Bioethics* 18(6): 473–92.

Bayer, R. and Stuber, J. (2008) Tobacco control, stigma, and public health: rethinking the relations. *American Journal of Public Health* 9(1): 47–50.

Becker, G. and Murphy, K. (1988) A theory of rational addiction. *Journal of Political Economy* 96(4): 675–700.

Begley, S. (2014) FDA calculates costs of lost enjoyment if e-cigarettes prevent smoking. *Reuters*, 2 June.

Begley, S. and Clarke, T. (2015) US to roll back 'lost pleasure' approach on health rules. *Reuters*, 18 March.

Bell, K., Salmon, A., Bowers, M., Bell, J. and McCullogh, L. (2010) Smoking, stigma and tobacco 'denormalization': further reflections on the use of stigma as a public health tool. A commentary on Social Science & Medicine's Stigma, Prejudice, Discrimination and Health Special Issue (67: 3). *Social Science and Medicine* 70(6): 795–99.

Berlin, I. (1969) *Four Essays on Liberty.* Oxford University Press.

Berridge, V. (2007) *Marketing Health: Smoking and the Discourse of Public Health in Britain, 1945–2000.* Oxford University Press.

Berridge, V. (2016) *Public Health: A Very Short Introduction.* Oxford University Press.

Bonell, C., McKee, M., Fletcher, A., Wilkinson, P. and Haines, A. (2011) One nudge forward, two steps back. *British Medical Journal* 342: 401.

Bonneux, L., Barendregt, J., Nusselder, W. and Van der Maas, P. (1998) Preventing fatal diseases increases healthcare costs: cause elimination life table approach. *British Medical Journal* 316: 26–29.

Borland, S. (2012) Just one small glass of wine a day raises a woman's risk of breast cancer. *Daily Mail*, 29 March.

Britton, J. (2015) Progress with global tobacco epidemic. *The Lancet* 385: 924–26.

Buchanan, D. (2008) Ethics in public health research. *American Journal of Public Health* 98(1): 15–21.

Burris, S. (2008) Stigma, ethics and policy: a commentary on Bayer's 'Stigma and ethics of public health: not can we but should we'. *Social Science and Medicine* 67: 473–75.

Callahan, D. (2013) Obesity: chasing the elusive epidemic. *Hastings Centre Report* 43(1): 34–40.

Campaign for Tobacco-Free Kids (n.d.) Increasing the minimum legal sale age for tobacco products to 21. https://www.tobaccofreekids.org/research/factsheets/pdf/0376.pdf

Campaign for Tobacco-Free Kids (2014) Top economists tell FDA its cost–benefit analyses of tobacco rules are badly flawed and underestimate benefits. http://www.tobaccofreekids.org/press_releases/post/2014_08_06_fda (6 August).

Campbell, D. (2016) Sugar tax: financially regressive but progressive for health? *Guardian*, 18 March.

Cantor, J., Torres, A., Abrams, C. and Elbe, B. (2015) Five years later: awareness of New York City's calorie labels declined, with no changes in calories purchased. *Health Affairs* 34(11): 1893–1900.

Capewell, S. (2014) Sugar sweetened drinks should carry obesity warning. *British Medical Journal* 348.

Carmona, R. (2003) *Can Tobacco Cure Smoking? A Review of Tobacco Harm Reduction*. Government Printing Office.

Cashmore, A. (2010) The Lucretian swerve: the biological basis of human behaviour and the criminal justice system. *Proceedings of the National Academy of Sciences* 107: 4499–504.

Cawley, J. (2011) The economics of obesity. In *The Oxford Handbook of the Social Science of Obesity* (ed. J. Cawley), pp. 120–37. Oxford University Press.

Chaloupka, F., Warner, K., Acemoglu, D., Gruber, J., Laux, F., Max, W., Newhouse, J., Schelleng, T. and Sindelar, J. (2014) An evaluation of the FDA's analysis of the costs and benefits of the graphic warning label regulation. *Tobacco Control* online first (30 December).

Chan, M. (2013) Opening address at the 8th Global Conference on Health Promotion, 10 June, Helsinki, Finland.

Chan, M. (2014) WHO Director-General's speech to the Regional Committee for the Western Pacific, 13 October.

Chapman, S. (2000) Banning smoking outdoors is seldom ethically justifiable. *Tobacco Control* 9: 95–97.

Chapman, S. and Freeman, B. (2008) Markers of the denormalisation of smoking and the tobacco industry. *Tobacco Control* 17: 25–31.

Charlton, B. (1995) A critique of Geoffrey Rose's 'population strategy' for preventive medicine. *Journal of the Royal Society of Medicine* 88: 607–10.

Childress, J., Faden, R., Gaare, R., Gostin, L., Kahn, J., Bonnie, R., Kass, N., Mastroianni, A., Moreno, J. and Nieburg, P. (2002) Public health ethics: mapping the terrain. *Journal of Law, Medicine and Ethics* 30: 170–78.

ComRes (2014) IEA lifestyle taxes poll. http://www.comres global.com/wp-content/uploads/2015/02/Lifestyle_taxes _Polling_Tables_December_20141.pdf

Conly, S. (2013) *Against Autonomy: Justifying Coercive Paternalism*. Cambridge University Press.

Conly, S. (2016) O*ne Child: Do We Have a Right to More?* Oxford University Press.

Deaton, A. and Cartwright, N. (2016) Understanding and misunderstanding randomised controlled trials. NBER Working Paper 22595.

Dworkin, R. (1971) Paternalism. In *Morality and the Law* (ed. R. Wasserstrom), pp. 181–88. Belmont: Wadsworth.

Edgley, C. and Brissett, D. (1990) Health Nazis and the cult of the perfect body: some polemical observations. *Symbolic Interaction* 13(2): 257–79.

Elbel, B., Gyamfi, J. and Kersh, R. (2011) Child and adolescent fast-food choice and the influence of calorie labelling: a natural experiment. *International Journal of Obesity* 35(4): 493–500.

Ellison, B., Luck, J. and Davis, D. (2014) The effect of calorie labels on caloric intake and restaurant revenue: evidence from two full-service restaurants. *Journal of Agricultural and Applied Economics* 46(2): 173–91.

Epstein, R. (2004) In defence of the 'old' public health: the legal framework for the regulation of public health. *Brooklyn Law Review*: 1421–70.

FCTC (2015) Conference of the Parties to the WHO Framework Convention on *Tobacco Control*: Sixth session. FCTC/COP/6/ VR.

FDA (2014) Food labeling: nutrition labeling of standard menu items in restaurants and similar retail food establishments. Final regulatory impact analysis, FDA-2011-F-0172.

Feinberg, J. (1971) Legal paternalism. *Canadian Journal of Philosophy* 1(1): 105–24.

Feinberg, J. (1984) *Harm to Others: The Moral Limits of the Criminal Law.* Oxford University Press.

Fitzpatrick, M. (2008) AIDS epidemic? It was a 'glorious myth'. *Spiked*, 5 September.

Gallet, C. and List, J. (2003) Cigarette demand: a meta-analysis of elasticities. *Health Economics* 12: 821–35.

General Lifestyle Survey (2013) *Smoking* (General Lifestyle Survey Overview – A Report on the 2011 General Lifestyle Survey). London: Office for National Statistics.

Gilmore, A., Savell, E. and Collin, J. (2011) Public health, corporations and the New Responsibility Deal: promoting partnerships with vectors of disease? *Journal of Public Health* 33(1): 2–4.

Gilpin, E., Lee, L. and Pierce, J. (2004) Changes in population attitudes about where smoking should not be allowed: California versus the rest of the USA. *Tobacco Control* 13: 38–44.

Glaeser, E. (2006) Paternalism and psychology. *University of Chicago Law Review* 73(1): 133–56.

Glantz, L. (2016) A commentary on Dean Galea's note. http://www.bu.edu/sph/2016/03/13/a-commentary-on-dean-galeas-note/ (13 March).

Glaze, B. (2016) David Cameron opens door to sugar tax on fizzy drinks. *Mirror*, 7 January.

Goodin, R. E. (1989) The ethics of smoking. *Ethics* 99(3): 574–624.

Gospodinov, N. and Irvine, I. (2004) Global health warnings on tobacco packaging: evidence from the Canadian experiment. *Topics in Economic Analysis & Policy* 4(1).

Gostin, L. (2013) Bloomberg's health legacy: urban innovator or meddling nanny? *Hastings Centre Report* 43(5): 19–25.

Gostin, L. and Gostin, K. (2009) A broader liberty: J. S. Mill, paternalism and the public's health. *Public Health* 123: 214–21.

Grill, K. and Voigt, K. (2015) The case for banning cigarettes. *Medical Ethics* 0: 1–9.

Halpern, D. (2015) *Inside the Nudge Unit*. London: WH Allen.

Hansard (1979) Road Traffic (Seat Belts) Bill. 22 March.

Hansard (2004) Protective Headgear for Young Cyclists Bill. 23 April.

Hansard (2006) Health Bill. 14 February.

Hansard (2013) Children and Families Bill. 20 November.

Hansard (2014) Draft Smoke-Free (Private Vehicles) Regulations 2015. 4 February.

Hansard (2015) Standardised Packaging of Tobacco Products Regulation 2015. 16 March.

Hausman, D. and Welch, B. (2010) Debate: to nudge or not to nudge. *Journal of Political Philosophy* 18(1): 123–36.

Hayek, F. (1945) The use of knowledge in society. *American Economic Review* 35(4): 519–30.

Health Survey for England (2016) Office for National Statistics. 14 December.

Herington, J., Dawson, A. and Draper, H. (2014) Obesity, liberty, and public health emergencies. *Hastings Centre Report* 4(6): 26–35.

Himmelfarb, G. (1987) Editor's introduction to *On Liberty* – see Mill (1987): 7–49.

Hiscock, R., Bauld, L., Amos, A. and Platt, S. (2012) Smoking and socioeconomic status in England: the rise of the never smoker and the disadvantaged smoker. *Journal of Public Health* 34(3): 390–96.

Hitchens, C. (2011) *The Quotable Hitchens: From Alcohol to Zionism*. Cambridge, MA: Da Capo Press.

HMRC (2016) Measuring tax gaps 2016 edition: tax gap estimates for 2014–15. 20 October.

Holmwood, L. (2006) ITV to end kids' TV production. *Guardian*, 20 June.

Holpuch, A. (2012) NYC soda ban hearing boisterous and heated – but public opinion absent. *Guardian*, 24 July.

Hospers, J. (1980) Libertarianism and legal paternalism. *Journal of Libertarian Studies* 4(3): 255–65.

Hyland, A., Li, Q., Bauer, J., Giovino, G., Steger, C. and Cummings, K. (2004) Predictors of cessation in a cohort of current and former smokers followed over 13 years. *Nicotine and Tobacco Research* 6 (Supp 3): S363–69.

Jacobsen, P. (2003) Safety in numbers: more walkers and bicyclists, safer walking and bicycling. *Injury Prevention* 9(3): 205–9.

Jepson, R., Harris, F., Platt, S. and Tannahill, C. (2010) The effectiveness of interventions to change six health behaviours: a review of reviews. *BMC Public Health* 10(538).

Jha, P. and Peto, R. (2013) Global effects of smoking, of quitting, and of taxing tobacco. *New England Journal of Medicine* 370: 60–68.

Kenkel, D., Mathios, A. and Wang, H. (2015) Menthol cigarette advertising and cigarette demand. NBER Working Paper 21790.

Kessler, D., Natanblut, S., Wilkenfeld, J., Lorraine, C., Mayl, S., Bernstein, I. and Thompson, L. (1997) Nicotine addiction: a paediatric disease. *Journal of Paediatrics* 130(4): 518–24.

Kirkham, E. (2015) 'Enjoying life to the fullest' is 2016's top resolution. *Time Money*, 31 December.

KPMG (2015) Project Sun: a study of the illicit cigarette market in the European Union, Norway and Switzerland.

Lancaster, K. and Lancaster, A. (2003) The economics of tobacco advertising: spending, demand, and the effects of bans. *International Journal of Advertising* 22(1): 41–65.

Lancet (2015) What will it take to create a tobacco-free world? 385(9972): 915.

Laux, F. L. (2000) Addiction as a market failure: using rational addiction results to justify tobacco regulation. *Journal of Health Economics* 19: 421–37.

Lawson, N. (1992) *The View from No. 11: Memoirs of a Tory Radical.* London: Bantam Press.

Lee, A. (2016) A healthy diet is cheaper than junk food but a good diet is still too expensive for some. *The Conversation*, 25 May. https://theconversation.com/a-healthy-diet-is-cheaper-than -junk-food-but-a-good-diet-is-still-too-expensive-for-some -57873

Le Grand, J. and New, B. (2015) *Government Paternalism: Nanny State or Helpful Friend?* Princeton University Press.

Leon, R. (2011) R. J. Reynolds v. US Food and Drug Administration. United States District Court for the District of Columbia. 7 November.

Leshner, G., Vultee, F., Bolls, P. and Moore, J. (2010) When fear isn't just a fear appeal: the effects of graphic anti-tobacco messages. *Journal of Broadcasting and Electronic Media* 54(3): 485–507.

Leshner, G., Bolls, P. and Wise, K. (2011) Motivated processing of fear appeal and disgust images in televised anti-tobacco ads. *Journal of Psychology: Theories, Methods, and Applications* 23(2): 77–89.

Levy, H., Norton, E. and Smith, J. (2016) Tobacco regulation and cost–benefit analysis: how should we value foregone consumer surplus? National Bureau of Economic Research Working Paper 22471.

Loprinzi, P., Branscum, A., Hanks, J. and Smit, E. (2016) Healthy lifestyle characteristics and their joint association with cardiovascular disease biomarkers in US adults. *Mayo Clinic Proceedings* 91(4): 432–42.

Lusk, J. and Rozan, A. (2008) Public policy and endogenous beliefs: the case of genetically modified food. *Journal of Agricultural and Resource Economics* 33(2): 270–89.

Lyons, R. and Snowdon, C. (2015) S*weet Truth: Is There a Market Failure in Sugar?* London: Institute of Economic Affairs.

Marteau, T., Ogilvie, D., Roland, M., Suhrcke, M. and Kelly, M. (2011) Judging nudging: can nudging improve population health? *British Medical Journal* 342: 262–65.

Marti, J. and Sindelar, J. (2015) Smaller cigarette pack as a commitment to smoke less? Insights from behavioural economics. *PLoS One* 10(9): e0137520.

McKee, M., Daube, M. and Chapman, S. (2016) E-cigarettes should be regulated. *Medical Journal of Australia* 204(9): 331.

Mill, J. S. (1987) *On Liberty.* London: Penguin.

Mill, J. S. (2004) *Principles of Political Economy with Some of Their Applications to Social Philosophy* (abridged). Indianapolis: Hackett.

Miller, D. (2010) *John Stuart Mill: Moral, Social, and Political Thought.* Cambridge: Polity.

Møller, L. and Matic, S. (2010) *Best Practice in Estimating the Costs of Alcohol – Recommendations for Future Studies.* Copenhagen: World Health Organization Europe.

Morrison, M. and Roese, N. (2011) Regrets of the typical American: findings from a nationally representative sample. *Social Psychological and Personality Science* 2(6): 567–83.

Muller, L., Lacroix, A., Luck, J. and Ruffleux, B. (2016) Distributional impacts of fat taxes and thin subsidies. *Economic Journal* 127(604): 2066–92.

Mussolini, B. and Gentile, G. (1932) The Doctrine of Fascism. https://archive.org/details/DoctrineOfFascism.

National Institutes of Health (2013) Improving cost–benefit analysis of tobacco regulation. Project Number 1R03CA 182990–01.

NIAID (National Institute of Allergy and Infectious Diseases) (2017) Appendum guidelines for the prevention of peanut allergy in the United States. US Department of Health and Human Services.

Nuffield Council on Bioethics (2007) *Public Health: Ethical Issues.* London: Nuffield Council on Bioethics.

Office for National Statistics (2009) Opinions Survey Report No. 40: Smoking-related behaviour and attitudes, 2008/09.

Office for National Statistics (2016a) Adult smoking habits in Great Britain: 2014. 18 February.

Office for National Statistics (2016b) Tobacco Bulletin. HM Revenue and Customs. 21 June.

Office for National Statistics (2016c) Alcohol Bulletin. HM Revenue and Customs. 29 July.

Parmet, W. (2014) Beyond paternalism: rethinking the limits of public health law. *Connecticut Law Review* 46(5): 1771–94.

Parry, L. (2015) Raising taxes on cigarettes by a THIRD would stop people smoking saving millions of lives. *Daily Mail*, 2 January.

Peele, S. (2016) Which is more addictive, coffee or nicotine? If you're asking, you can't understand the answer. *The Influence* http://theinfluence.org/which-is-more-addictive-coffee-or -nicotine-if-youre-asking-you-cant-understand-the-answer/.

Petrescu, D., Vasiljevic, M., Pepper, J., Ribisl, K. and Marteau, T. (2016) What is the impact of e-cigarette adverts on children's perceptions of tobacco smoking? An experimental study. *Tobacco Control* doi:10.1136/tobaccocontrol-2016–052940.

Phillips, C. (2016a) The weakness of ethical thinking in public health: a case study. https://antithrlies.com/2016/06/06/the -weakness-of-ethical-thinking-in-public-health-a-case-study/ (6 June).

Phillips, C. (2016b) What harm reduction really means. https:// antithrlies.com/2016/08/05/what-harm-reduction-really -means/ (5 August).

Phillips, C. (2016c) *Understanding the Basic Economics of Tobacco Harm Reduction*. London: Institute of Economic Affairs.

Ploug, T., Holm, S. and Gjerris, M. (2015) The stigmatization dilemma in public health policy – the case of MRSA in Denmark. *BMC Public Health* 15: 640.

Prieto, L. and Sacristán, J. (2003) Problems and solutions in calculating quality-adjusted life years (QALYs). *Health and Quality of Life Outcomes* 1(80).

Public Health England (2015) Sugar reduction: the evidence for action. October.

Public Health England (2016) Annual report and accounts (2015/16). 21 July.

Qi, S. (2013) The impact of advertising regulation on industry: the cigarette advertising ban of 1971. *Rand Journal of Economics* 44(2): 215–48.

Radcliffe, D. (2014) For policy discouraging smoking, FDA defies common sense in weighing 'lost pleasure' against benefits. *Huffington Post*, 29 August.

Rappange, D., Brouwer, W., Rutten, F. and van Baal, P. (2010) Lifestyle intervention: from cost savings to value for money. *Journal of Public Health* 32(3): 440–47.

Robertson, T. and Rossiter, J. (1974) Children and commercial persuasion: an attribution theory analysis. *Journal of Consumer Research* 1: 13–20.

Robinson, D. (1996) Head injuries and bicycle helmet laws. *Accident Analysis & Prevention* 28(4): 463–75.

Robinson, D. (2006) Do enforced bicycle helmet laws improve public health? *British Medical Journal* 332(7545): 722–25.

Rose, G. (2008) *Rose's Strategy of Preventive Medicine*. Oxford University Press.

Rothstein, M. (2009) The limits of public health: a response. *Public Health Ethics* 2(1): 84–88.

Royal College of Physicians (2016) *Nicotine without Smoke*. London: Royal College of Physicians.

Russell, L. (2009) Preventing chronic disease: an important investment, but don't count on cost savings. *Health Affairs* 28 (1): 42–45.

Schudson, M. (1993) *Advertising: The Uneasy Persuasion*. London: Routledge.

Scruton, R. (2015) *Fools, Frauds and Firebrands: Thinkers of the New Left*. London: Bloomsbury.

Seedhouse, D. (2016) The NHS has banned cigarettes and should ban meat too – both cause cancer. *The Guardian*, 3 September.

Simon, J. (1970) *Issues in the Economics of Advertising*. Urbana: University of Illinois Press.

Singh, T., Agaku, I., Arrazola, R., Marynak, K., Neff, L., Rolle, I. and King, B. (2016) Exposure to advertisements and electronic cigarette use among US middle and high school students. *Paediatrics* 137(5).

Smith, A. (2013) 60% of cigarettes sold in New York are smuggled: report. *CNN Money*, 10 January.

Snowdon, C. (2011) *The Art of Suppression: Panic, Pleasure and Prohibition since 1800*. Ripon: Little Dice.

Snowdon, C. (2012a) *Drinking in the Shadow Economy*. London: Institute of Economic Affairs.

Snowdon, C. (2012b) *Sock Puppets: How the Government Lobbies Itself and Why*. London: Institute of Economic Affairs.

Snowdon, C. (2014) *The Sock Doctrine*. London: Institute of Economic Affairs.

Snowdon, C. (2015a) *Alcohol and the Public Purse*. London: Institute of Economic Affairs.

Snowdon, C. (2015b) *Drinking, Fast and Slow*. London: Institute of Economic Affairs.

Snowdon, C. (2017) *Rational Alcohol Taxation* (briefing). London: Institute of Economic Affairs.

Snyder, L., Milici, F., Slater, M., Sun, H. and Strizhakova, Y. (2006) Effects of alcohol advertising exposure on drinking among youth. *Archives of Paediatrics and Adolescent Medicine Journal* 160(1): 18–24.

Song, A., Brown, P. and Glantz, S. (2014) When health policy and empirical evidence collide: the case of cigarette package warning labels and economic consumer surplus. *American Journal of Public Health* 104(2): e42–51.

Stern, A. M. (2005) Sterilised in the name of public health: race, immigration, and reproductive control in modern California. *American Journal of Public Health* 95(7): 1128–38.

Sugden, R. (2016) Do people really want to be nudged towards healthy lifestyles? *International Review of Economics* doi:10.1007/s12232–016–0264–1.

Sullum, J. (1998) *For Your Own Good: The Anti-Smoking Crusade and the Tyranny of Public Health*. New York: The Free Press.

Sundborn, G., Thornley, S., Te Morenga, L. and Merriman, T. (2014) FIZZ sugary drink free Pacific by 2030 – Symposium Declaration. *New Zealand Medical Journal* 127(1392): 98–101.

Sunstein, C. (2014a) *Why Nudge?* New Haven: Yale University Press.

Sunstein, C. (2014b) *Simpler: The Future of Government*. New York: Simon and Schuster.

Sunstein, C. (2017) On mandatory labeling, with special reference to genetically modified foods. *University of Pennsylvania Law Review* 165(5): 1043–95.

Taxpayers' Alliance (2016) The nanny state rich list, 4 August.

Thaler, R. and Sunstein, C. (2008) *Nudge: Improving Decisions about Health, Wealth, and Happiness*. London: Penguin.

Tovey, M. (2017) *Obesity and the Public Purse*. London: Institute of Economic Affairs.

Universum (2015) Understanding a misunderstood generation.

Van der Eijk (2015) Ethics of tobacco harm reduction from a liberal perspective. *Journal of Medical Ethics* doi:10.1136/medethics-2015-102974.

Van der Zee, T., Anaya, J. and Brown, N. (2017) Statistical heartburn: an attempt to digest four pizza publications from the Cornell Food and Brand Lab. *PeerJPreprints* https://doi.org/10.7287/peerj.preprints.2748v1

Viscusi, W. and Hakes, J. (2008) Risk beliefs and smoking behaviour. *Economic Inquiry* 46(1): 45–59.

Wagenaar, A., Salois, M. and Komro, K. (2009) Effects of beverage alcohol price and tax levels on drinking: a meta-analysis of 1003 estimates from 112 studies. *Addiction* 104: 179–90.

Wakefield, M., Coomber, K., Zacher, M., Durkin, S., Brennan, E. and Scollo, M. (2014) Australian adult smokers' responses to plain packaging with larger graphic health warnings 1 year after implementation: results from a national cross-sectional tracking survey. *Tobacco Control* 24: ii17–ii25.

Wansink, B. (2015) Change their choice! Changing behaviour using the CAN approach and activism research. *Psychology and Marketing* 32: 486–500.

Wardlaw, M. (2004) Effectiveness of cycle helmets and the ethics of legislation. *Journal of the Royal Society of Medicine* 97(8): 409–10.

Wardle, H., Pickup, D., Lee, L., Hall, J., Pickering, K., Grieg, K., Moodie, C. and MacKintosh, A. (2010) *Evaluating the Impact of Picture Health Warnings on Cigarette Packets.* Public Health Research Consortium.

West, R. and Marteau, T. (2013) Commentary on Casswell (2013): The commercial determinants of health. *Addiction* 108(4): 686–87.

Whyte, J. (2013) *Quack Policy: Abusing Science in the Cause of Paternalism*. London: Institute of Economic Affairs.

Wilcox, G., Kang, E. and Chilek, L. (2015) Beer, wine, or spirits? Advertising's impact on four decades of category sales. *International Journal of Advertising* 34(4): 641–57.

Wiley, L. (2012) Rethinking the new public health. *Washington and Lee Law Review* 69(1): 207–72.

Wiley, L., Berman, M. and Blanke, D. (2013) Who's your nanny? Choice, paternalism and public health in the age of personal responsibility. *Journal of Law, Medicine and Ethics* 41(s1): 88–91.

Wilson, J. (2011) Why it's time to stop worrying about paternalism in health policy. *Public Health Ethics* 4(3): 269–79.

Yasin, J. (1995) The effect of advertising in fast-moving consumer goods markets. *International Journal of Advertising* 14(2): 133–47.

INDEX

ABOUT THE IEA

The Institute is a research and educational charity (No. CC 235 351), limited by guarantee. Its mission is to improve understanding of the fundamental institutions of a free society by analysing and expounding the role of markets in solving economic and social problems.

The IEA achieves its mission by:

- a high-quality publishing programme
- conferences, seminars, lectures and other events
- outreach to school and college students
- brokering media introductions and appearances

The IEA, which was established in 1955 by the late Sir Antony Fisher, is an educational charity, not a political organisation. It is independent of any political party or group and does not carry on activities intended to affect support for any political party or candidate in any election or referendum, or at any other time. It is financed by sales of publications, conference fees and voluntary donations.

In addition to its main series of publications, the IEA also publishes (jointly with the University of Buckingham), *Economic Affairs*.

The IEA is aided in its work by a distinguished international Academic Advisory Council and an eminent panel of Honorary Fellows. Together with other academics, they review prospective IEA publications, their comments being passed on anonymously to authors. All IEA papers are therefore subject to the same rigorous independent refereeing process as used by leading academic journals.

IEA publications enjoy widespread classroom use and course adoptions in schools and universities. They are also sold throughout the world and often translated/reprinted.

Since 1974 the IEA has helped to create a worldwide network of 100 similar institutions in over 70 countries. They are all independent but share the IEA's mission.

Views expressed in the IEA's publications are those of the authors, not those of the Institute (which has no corporate view), its Managing Trustees, Academic Advisory Council members or senior staff.

Members of the Institute's Academic Advisory Council, Honorary Fellows, Trustees and Staff are listed on the following page.

The Institute gratefully acknowledges financial support for its publications programme and other work from a generous benefaction by the late Professor Ronald Coase.

Other books recently published by the IEA include:

New Private Monies – A Bit-Part Player?
Kevin Dowd
Hobart Paper 174; ISBN 978–0–255–36694–6; £10.00

From Crisis to Confidence – Macroeconomics after the Crash
Roger Koppl
Hobart Paper 175; ISBN 978–0–255–36693–9; £12.50

Advertising in a Free Society
Ralph Harris and Arthur Seldon
With an introduction by Christopher Snowdon
Hobart Paper 176; ISBN 978–0–255–36696–0; £12.50

Selfishness, Greed and Capitalism: Debunking Myths about the Free Market
Christopher Snowdon
Hobart Paper 177; ISBN 978–0–255–36677–9; £12.50

Waging the War of Ideas
John Blundell
Occasional Paper 131; ISBN 978–0–255–36684–7; £12.50

Brexit: Directions for Britain Outside the EU
Ralph Buckle, Tim Hewish, John C. Hulsman, Iain Mansfield and
Robert Oulds
Hobart Paperback 178; ISBN 978–0–255–36681–6; £12.50

Flaws and Ceilings – Price Controls and the Damage They Cause
Edited by Christopher Coyne and Rachel Coyne
Hobart Paperback 179; ISBN 978–0–255–36701–1; £12.50

*Scandinavian Unexceptionalism: Culture, Markets and the Failure of
Third-Way Socialism*
Nima Sanandaji
Readings in Political Economy 1; ISBN 978–0–255–36704–2; £10.00

Classical Liberalism – A Primer
Eamonn Butler
Readings in Political Economy 2; ISBN 978–0–255–36707–3; £10.00

Federal Britain: The Case for Decentralisation
Philip Booth
Readings in Political Economy 3; ISBN 978–0–255–36713–4; £10.00

Forever Contemporary: The Economics of Ronald Coase
Edited by Cento Veljanovski
Readings in Political Economy 4; ISBN 978–0–255–36710–3; £15.00

Power Cut? How the EU Is Pulling the Plug on Electricity Markets
Carlo Stagnaro
Hobart Paperback 180; ISBN 978–0–255–36716–5; £10.00

Policy Stability and Economic Growth – Lessons from the Great Recession
John B. Taylor
Readings in Political Economy 5; ISBN 978–0–255–36719–6; £7.50

Breaking Up Is Hard To Do: Britain and Europe's Dysfunctional Relationship
Edited by Patrick Minford and J. R. Shackleton
Hobart Paperback 181; ISBN 978–0–255–36722–6; £15.00

In Focus: The Case for Privatising the BBC
Edited by Philip Booth
Hobart Paperback 182; ISBN 978–0–255–36725–7; £12.50

Islamic Foundations of a Free Society
Edited by Nouh El Harmouzi and Linda Whetstone
Hobart Paperback 183; ISBN 978–0–255–36728–8; £12.50

The Economics of International Development: Foreign Aid versus Freedom for the World's Poor
William Easterly
Readings in Political Economy 6; ISBN 978–0–255–36731–8; £7.50

Taxation, Government Spending and Economic Growth
Edited by Philip Booth
Hobart Paperback 184; ISBN 978–0–255–36734–9; £15.00

Universal Healthcare without the NHS: Towards a Patient-Centred Health System
Kristian Niemietz
Hobart Paperback 185; ISBN 978–0–255–36737–0; £10.00

Sea Change: How Markets and Property Rights Could Transform the Fishing Industry
Edited by Richard Wellings
Readings in Political Economy 7; ISBN 978–0–255–36740–0; £10.00

Working to Rule: The Damaging Economics of UK Employment Regulation
J. R. Shackleton
Hobart Paperback 186; ISBN 978–0–255–36743–1; £15.00

Education, War and Peace: The Surprising Success of Private Schools in War-Torn Countries
James Tooley and David Longfield
ISBN 978–0–255–36746–2; £10.00

Other IEA publications

Comprehensive information on other publications and the wider work of the IEA can be found at www.iea.org.uk. To order any publication please see below.

Personal customers

Orders from personal customers should be directed to the IEA:

Clare Rusbridge
IEA
2 Lord North Street
FREEPOST LON10168
London SW1P 3YZ
Tel: 020 7799 8907. Fax: 020 7799 2137
Email: sales@iea.org.uk

Trade customers

All orders from the book trade should be directed to the IEA's distributor:

NBN International (IEA Orders)
Orders Dept.
NBN International
10 Thornbury Road
Plymouth PL6 7PP
Tel: 01752 202301, Fax: 01752 202333
Email: orders@nbninternational.com

IEA subscriptions

The IEA also offers a subscription service to its publications. For a single annual payment (currently £42.00 in the UK), subscribers receive every monograph the IEA publishes. For more information please contact:

Clare Rusbridge
Subscriptions
IEA
2 Lord North Street
FREEPOST LON10168
London SW1P 3YZ
Tel: 020 7799 8907, Fax: 020 7799 2137
Email: crusbridge@iea.org.uk